MARKETING PRACTICES IN SMALL-SCALE INDUSTRIES

MARKETING PRACTICES IN SMALL-SCALE INDUSTRIES

R.P. HOODA

Faculty of Commerce & Management
Kurukshetra University
Haryana

HERITAGE PUBLISHERS
NEW DELHI 1991

ISBN 81-7026-168-6

Published by B.R. Chawla, Heritage Publishers, Ansari Road, Daryaganj, New Delhi-110 002. Laser Typeset by Mac Printec, 84 Darya Ganj, New Delhi-110 002 and Printed at Cambridge Printing Works, B-85, Naraina Phase II, New Delhi-110 028.

Contents

Preface vii – ix

I **INTRODUCTION** 1 – 12

II **SAMPLE UNITS: A PROFILE** 13 – 25

Form of Organization and Asset Size-groups 13

Form of Organization and Product-groups 15

Age of Sample Units 17

Capital Invested 20

Size of Employment 22

III **PRODUCT PLANNING AND DEVELOPMENT** 26 – 45

Product Mix 27

Product Development 30

Product Standardization 34

Branding 37

Packaging 40

Objectives of Packaging 43

IV **PRICING POLICIES AND PRACTICES** 46 – 62

Objectives of Pricing 47

Factors Influencing Price Setting 49

Pricing Policies 52

Price Charged in Relation to Competitors' Prices 54

Factors Leading to Price Changes 57

Discounts Offered 60

V **ADVERTISING, PERSONAL SELLING AND SALES PROMOTION** 63 – 89

Relative Importance of the Three Components 64

Promotional Expenses in Relation to Sales 66

	Advertising	70
	Methods of Deciding Advertising Budget	70
	Advertising Objectives	72
	Advertising Media Used	74
	Preparation of Advertising Message	78
	Advertising Coverage	80
	Personal Selling	83
	Sales Force Functions	85
	Sales Promotion	87
VI	**CHANNEL DECISIONS**	90 - 103
	Channel Levels	91
	Distribution Intensity	94
	Factors Affecting the Selection of Middlemen	97
	Motivating Middlemen	100
VII	**SOME OTHER ISSUES**	104 - 119
	Sales Forecasting	104
	Market Segmentation—Geographical Coverage	108
	Credit Facilities to Buyers	111
	Inventory	114
	Elements of Marketing Mix—Relative Importance	116
VIII	**FINDINGS**	120 - 137
	Implications	134
	Annexure—Questionnaire	*139 - 148*
	Bibliography	*149 - 152*
	Index	*153*

Preface

The small-scale industries have played a significant role in India's economic development since the commencement of the First Five year Plan. The resources being scarce and with no respite from high population growth rate, the small industry sector will continue to be increasingly relevant in determining the future pace of economic development for a long time to come. The fact that this sector covers a wide variety of manufacturing units differing in terms of products, size and scale of operations, technology employed, and the form of organization, makes it abundantly crucial in its overall contribution to solving some of the burning problems facing the Indian economy.

The small-scale industrial scene in India has undergone a sea change in terms of physical expansion, geographical spread and spectrum of business activities especially over the past few years. This sector is adding as many as 5,000 products to the basket of national production which are being produced in about 16 lac registered and 5 lac unregistered units. The output varies from simple consumer goods like soaps and shoes to the most sophisticated goods like electronics, electro-medical/surgical items, and microwave equipment. According to the latest estimate, the small-scale units employ more than 1.4 crore persons, contribute 50 per cent of the value of the entire manufacturing output, and account for 27 per cent of the total export value.

Even after having attained a place of so much prominence

in the national economy, the small manufacturing units continue to face a number of marketing problems. Lack of market intelligence, absence of market research and feedback, weak marketing network, and, above all, inadequate knowledge of modern marketing techniques have made their growth prospects highly disquietening. The very survival and future growth of these units vis-a-vis the medium and large scale units, depend essentially on the kind of activities which go into the formation of their marketing strategy. Indeed, no better performance can be expected of them unless they improve their marketing efforts, and strive to be competitive in the adoption of modern marketing practices. An essential prerequisite for achieving this, is to gain knowledge about the marketing practices and policies which are currently being followed by them in the area of production, pricing, promotion, and distribution. And the present study is a humble attempt precisely in this very direction.

Though the study is based on the analysis of sample data collected from the small-scale industries located in the state of Haryana, its findings are quite general in their application. The reason being that, taking Haryana as the only state randomly selected at the first stage of sampling, the units actually selected in the sample are by all means representative of the entire small-scale sector at the national level. This is true also because a majority of units in the small-scale sector, irrespective of their location in a particular state, shares common characteristics and problems. There are, indeed, very specific reasons for the sample units being selected from those located in Haryana. Apart from the various points stated in the Chapter on Introduction, the locational and other advantages available to the small industries in Haryana make them the most ideally suited lot for a sample study on marketing practices characteristic of these industries in general.

The development of small industry has emerged as a powerful movement throughout the country during the last two decades. The fiscal and other incentives jointly provided by the central and state governments have contributed significantly to the sharp rise in the number of small units. The role played by the Haryana government is particularly worthy of praise, for some of the steps initiated have worked as a bonanza in attracting budding small entrepreneurs. It is in this background that the findings of this study are considered to be highly useful in terms of their implications for the growth prospects of the small industrial sector in general, especially because its market growth is impeded by the non-adoption of even simple principles of marketing.

Time and money are always the abiding constraints in undertaking survey-based research work of this kind. Recognising its usefulness, and in its endeavour to promote socially relevant research, the University Grants Commission (UGC) accepted the research proposal submitted in this behalf and agreed to extend necessary financial assistance to carry it out. Had the requisite funds not been made available, undertaking the present study would have been extremely difficult. No words of gratitude would suffice to match their generosity.

The readiness with which the respondents from the small-scale sector parted with the needed information has been a pleasant experience all through. Shri Bhag Singh Bodla, who worked as a Research Fellow for the major part of the duration of this study, deserves appreciation for his streneous efforts in getting the questionnaire filled at personal level, and subsequently processing and appropriately presenting the data with dedication. Mention must also be made of the benefits of having had fruitful discussions with my colleagues, especially Dr S. C. Davar, in the department.

R. P. Hooda

Chapter I

Introduction

Industrialization plays a crucial role in the process of economic development. Its character and direction assume special significance in developing countries like India. National income, per capita income, output, and employment can grow at a faster rate only through development of industries of various sizes. Small-scale industrial sector deserves priority as an instrument of industrialization, especially in those economies which are facing the problem of population explosion. Although large and medium industries also generate employment opportunities, they require comparatively heavier amount of capital, which is generally scarce. Shortage of capital being a chronic problem in developing countries, it has to be utilized most efficiently on a selective basis in various income-employment generating activities.

By their very nature small-scale industrial units require much less capital. As they are relatively more labour-intensive, they generate more jobs per unit of investment than the medium and large industries do. According to an estimate given in the World Bank Report,[1] the amount of capital required for creation of a single job in small units is only one third of that required in large scale industries.

India has accepted a socialistic pattern of society as the

1. Phillip A Meek, Small Enterprises Development Policies and Programme, *Management Development Services*, No. 14, ILO, Geneva (1977), p. 71.

cherished goal of economic development. It implies, among other things, equitable distribution of income and reduction in the concentration of economic power. One of the distinctive advantages of expansion of the small-scale industrial sector is that it serves as an effective weapon in the hands of the government to achieve these objectives. Regional disparities in the growth rates of industrial output and per capita income can be substantially reduced by setting up small-scale units in the industrially backward areas by creating the needed infrastructural facilities. Standard of living of the rural population can also be easily raised by encouraging establishment of such units in the rural areas. However, this would require provision for the much needed managerial, technical, and marketing facilities.

Keeping in view these advantages, the Industrial Policy Resolution of 1948 took adequate notice of the suitability of small-scale industries for better utilization of local resources and for meeting the local demand for many types of consumer goods. The small industry sector, therefore, received due emphasis during the various Five Year Plans. The First Plan witnessed the creation of a number of All India level boards (including Khadi and Village Industries Board). The National Small Industries Corporation was also established during this plan to enhance the marketability of the output of small-scale industries. The Plan envisaged an outlay of Rs. 43 crores for the development of these industries. In the Second Plan emphasis was laid on the development of small-scale industries and ancillaries to large scale industries, and on organizing industrial cooperatives. An amount of Rs. 175 crores was earmarked for the development of these industries. This constituted 3.8 per cent of the total plan outlay.

The trend continued with a provision of Rs. 264 crores (3.1 per cent of the total plan outlay) for the development of small-scale sector during the Third Plan. The three Annual Plans (1966-67, 1967-68, and 1968-69) also witnessed the development of a number of industrial estates. With an actual expenditure of Rs. 251 crores on the development of this sector during the Fourth Plan, the list of items reserved for production in the small-scale sector increased from 180 to 504. The number of such items again increased to 807 during the Fifth Plan, which envisaged an expenditure of Rs. 510 crores on the development of this sector.

With an outlay of Rs. 1410 crores (1.4 per cent of the total plan outlay), the Sixth Plan further reiterated the resolve to step up the process of development and modernization of these industries. To ensure rapid growth, the definition of small-scale industries and ancillaries was revised, raising the investment limit to Rs. 20 lac for small-scale units and Rs. 25 lac for ancillaries. The launching of the Seventh Plan in 1985 witnessed a further revision of these limits to Rs. 35 lac for small-scale industries and Rs. 45 lac for ancillaries. Inspite of the fact that the small-scale industrial sector had received priority all through the Plans, the allocations made for this sector as proportion of total plan outlays have followed a declining trend ever since the Second Plan.

Various industrial policy resolutions adopted from time to time also reflect clearly the tilt in favour of the growth of small-scale industries. To begin with, the Industrial Policy Statement of 6 April 1948 clearly brought out the status accorded to small and cottage industries as under:

> Cottage and small-scale industries have a very important role in the national economy, offering as they do scope for individual, village or cooperative enterprises, and means for the rehabilitation of displaced persons.

The Industrial Policy Resolution of 1956 added a new dimension to the basic approach towards this sector insofar as it stipulated the establishment of industrial estates and rural workshops, and making adequate provision for requisite financial and technical help. The Industrial Policy Statement of 1977 had its main thrust on effective promotion of cottage and small industries and their wide dispersal in rural areas and small towns. It emphasized the setting up of District

Industries Centres to provide all facilities to small-scale entrepreneurs under the same roof. The Industrial Policy Statement of 1980 emphasized the need for continuation of marketing support to the decentralized sector and reservation of items for production by the small-scale industries sector. It proposed an increase in the number of items reserved for exclusive manufacture in the small-scale sector to 833, which was further raised to 872 in March 1984.

As a result of consistent bias in favour of development of small-scale industries, they have now come to occupy an important place in the Indian economy, which is expected to be maintained in the decades to come. While assessing the place of these industries in the Indian context, one is often faced with the problem of paucity of adequate and reliable data. This is primarily because of their heterogeneous character, and the fact that all of them are not registered with the various data collecting agencies. Inspite of such difficulties, the industries departments of each State compile district-wise annual data on the small-scale sector in respect of number of units, production, employment, capital investment, exports, etc.

The analysis of these data at the national level shows that the performance of small-scale industries has indeed been impressive. The total number of units increased from 4.98 lac in 1974-75 to 11.50 lac in 1983-84. The value of fixed investment rose to Rs. 7360 crores in 1983-84 from Rs. 2697 crores in 1974-75. Total production in value terms has gone up to Rs. 41620 crores in 1983-84 as against Rs. 9200 crores in 1974-75. The total number of persons employed in this sector which was 6.7 lac in 1960 increased to 84 lac in 1983-84. Moreover, these industries have also not lagged behind even in terms of their contribution to exports. Exports from small industries reached the mark of Rs. 2159 crores in 1983-84 as compared to Rs. 541 crores in 1974-75. According to the latest statistics given in the Economic Survey of 1986-87, there were 13.53 lac units of small size at the end of December 1986, providing employment to 96 lac persons, generating gross output valued at Rs. 61,000 crores, and accounting for 22.5 per cent of total exports.

Inspite of excellent performance, these industries are facing a number of chronic problems in the areas of finance, production and, particularly, marketing. To ensure that the growth of these industries does not suffer due to various problems in these key areas, the Central as well as the State Governments have initiated and implemented a number of new programmes aimed at solving them. Yet the growth rate of these industries has not been commensurate with the amount of efforts made. Even those units which had been established long ago do not find themselves capable of undertaking expansion and modernization of their production facilities. While many have closed down, others have fallen sick and are on the verge of a collapse.

Lack of demand for their products is one of the most serious problems facing these industries. Owing to the small size, they lack the funds needed for market argumentation. Many of them have also to face stiff competition from large scale industries. Apart from their capability to conduct market surveys before undertaking the production of any item, large scale industries use more sophisticated techniques of production, spend large sums of money on advertising and publicity, and use other modern marketing practices to make their products saleable. Small-scale units, on the other hand, are neither capable of using sophisticated production techniques and conducting market surveys, nor are they in a position to spend huge funds on advertisement and publicity. To distribute their products to the final users, they have to depend on the mercy of middlemen. Charging middlemen's margin to production costs makes the products produced in the small sector costlier than those manufactured by the large scale industries.

Since most of the small sector units are run either on partnership or proprietorship basis and the owners are relatively less educated, many of them are not even aware of the modern techniques of marketing such as product development, brand promotion, packaging, advertising, market surveys, and demand forecasts. This acts as a serious impediment in their growth because small entrepreneurs fail to reap the advantages of market creation and image-building, which cannot be possible without the adoption of modern marketing practices. It is in recognition of this need that the Working Group on small-scale industries recommended undertaking of market surveys and market research. The present study is an attempt in that direction with the main purpose of bringing out the marketing practices prevalent in these industries.

Selection of the State of Haryana for taking up this study was not a matter of convenience only. There were specific reasons for considering Haryana as the most suited for the purpose. At one time a backward region of the erstwhile Punjab, Haryana now is one of the leading go-ahead states which has made tremendous all-round progress since its inception on November 1, 1966. So fast has been its growth rate that in a relatively short period it has come to be known as the most developed State in India, second only to Punjab. Having made rapid strides in the field of agriculture, it did not lag behind in creating an excellent infrastructure for industrial growth. Its proximity to the national capital city of New Delhi enabled it to make added gains in the form of ready market for raw materials, finished goods, and trading etc. Under the impetus provided by all these factors, the number of industrial units of all sizes has increased manifold. In addition to five units in the central public sector, at present the number of large and medium units in the State is 387 with a very wide and diverse product base. Notable among the major products/items manufactured are tractors, automobiles, earth-moving machinery, motor cycles, bicycles, air conditioners, sanitary wares, textile products, etc. Among the highlights, about 25 per cent of India's total production of sanitary wares, and one out of every four bicycles in the country, are manufactured in Haryana. It is no less laudable an achievement that its index of industrial production has now risen to a level considerably higher than the All India average.

A significant feature of industrial development in Haryana is the fast growth experienced by the small-scale industrial sector which has emerged as a powerful movement in the State over a period of 22 years. From 4500 units in 1966 when Haryana was born, the number of small-scale units has crossed the mark of 83,100 units in 1988-89. Today many of these units are equipped with modern machines and are engaged in manufacturing a wide range of products, including light engineering items, scientific instruments, auto-parts, agricultural implements, handloom products, gas stoves, ammunition boxes, electrical mixies, etc. The small-scale units at Ambala meet about 20 per cent of India's total export of scientific instruments. Those at Yamuna Nagar cater to about 60 per cent of the demand for ammunition boxes by the country's armed forces. The units located at Panipat supply 75 per cent of the total requirement of woollen blankets for the Indian Army. And, amazingly enough, all this is being done in the small-scale sector. It is in view of these points that Haryana has a justifiable claim to be the obvious choice for undertaking any study on this sector in any area whether production, finance, or marketing. The overall structure and the performance of small-scale industries in the state during recent years can yield special advantages for an investigation, particularly in the marketing area.

Since it is a study of the marketing practices of small-scale industries, it has been undertaken primarily with a view to examine the policies and practices relating to product, price, distribution, promotion, and other matters related to marketing. This will also help bring out the modern marketing practices which are being followed, and those which have failed to receive acceptance by the small firms. Within the overall framework of these objectives, some of the broad hypotheses which it seeks to verify during the course of analysis are as follows :

a) Product development activity is very low and production is often undertaken without much regard to market needs.
b) Majority of manufacturers sell their products without using brand name and quality mark.
c) Packaging is considered more as a means of product protection and convenience in handling than as a means of promotion.
d) Generally pricing decisions are taken in keeping with the competitive factors. Price is more frequently used as a tool of increasing sales and meeting competition.
e) Majority of the small entrepreneurs make their products available to the final consumers through middlemen, whose selection is governed mainly by the consideration of goodwill than by anything else.
f) A positive, though not very significant, relationship exists between promotion expenses and sales.
g) Use of inexpensive advertising media is more popular and most of the small-scale units do not get advertising message prepared from specialized agencies.
h) Personal selling is the least important element of marketing mix, most prominent being the use of many odd sales promotion activities.

The study is based on two-way analysis of sample data on each aspect: first in terms of three size-groups, and then in terms of five product-groups. This has been done not as an analytical exercise, but also for the sake of the refinements it adds to the discussion. As small, medium, and large are the three size-groups, the analysis according to these size-groups introduces the element of size within small size which enables us to bring out a comparative picture among various size-groups. The purpose is to highlight the similarities and dissimilarities in the use of marketing practices in the three size-groups and to identify the pattern of variations therein. Going by the definition of small-scale industries given by the Haryana Government, to be stated later, the three size-groups have been delineated on the basis of the value of fixed investment in plant and machinery as under:

i) *Small size-group:* Consisting of units with investment valued at Rs. 2 lac or less.
ii) *Medium size-group:* Consisting of units with investment valued at more than Rs. 2 lac, but less than Rs. 7 lac.
iii) *Large size-group:* Consisting of units with investment valued at Rs. 7 lac, but not exceeding Rs. 45 lac.

The analysis in terms of different product-groups further adds to the analytical value of the discussion. Again, the purpose is to highlight the similarities and dissimilarities in the marketing practices followed by the units manufacturing different products. The product items covered under each of the five product-groups are as follows :

I. *Chemicals :* Chemicals and chemical products, rubber plastic, and paints.
II. *Textiles :* Cotton textiles, wool, silk, synthetic fibre, textiles, including jute and mesta textiles.
III. *Engineering :* Agricultural implements, scientific instruments, electrical machinery, transport equipments, and parts thereof.
IV. *Metals :* Steel furniture, potteries, utensils, building material, and other metal and non-metal products.
V. *Food-Wood :* Food products, wood and wood products, wooden furniture, printing, and publishing material.

It may be noticed that the grouping of different products under the five product-groups has been made more on functional basis than technical. It would have been more appropriate to have a few more product-groups to avoid too much jumbling of diverse products under one group. The food-wood product group, for example, is the case in point. But we refrained from doing so because it would have made the analysis unduly lengthy and complex without adding much to its analytical value.

The analysis is based on primary data collected from small-scale units located and registered in the State of Haryana. At the time when data collection was being planned, industrial units with an investment of Rs. 35 lac or less in plant and machinery (Rs. 45 lac in the case of ancillaries) had been declared by the Government as small-scale units. These data were obtained during January-March 1988 through a pre-tested well designed questionnaire, which is given in Annexure-I. It consisted of questions covering all significant marketing activities with a view to seeking the desired information falling in the following categories :

i) general information about the sample units,
ii) product related information,
iii) price related information,
iv) distribution related information, and
v) promotional activities related information.

Most of the questions were multiple-choice questions and made close-ended to ensure objectivity in data collection and analysis.

The questionnaire was administered to the owner of the unit selected in the sample or, in his absence, to a responsible person aware of the working of the unit and deputed by the owner for the purpose. The questionnaire was distributed to the respondents in advance to allow them sufficient time for careful reading. To have them finally filled up, each respondent was approached personally by the investigator who provided necessary clarifications whenever needed. During the course of interview, cross-questions were also raised by the investigator, yielding additional information of useful nature. This enabled us to achieve the desired degree of reliability and accuracy in data collection.

The sample was selected by using the (proportionate) stratified random sampling technique. Taking all small-scale units listed in the Directory for the year 1981-82 published by the Haryana State Small-Scale Industries and Export Corporation as the universe, the entire universe was divided into 12 strata according to geographical area (district-wise stratification). To give due representation to each district, approximately 2.5% of the target population units in each district were selected in the sample. In all, 400 units were selected, whose distribution is as given in Table 1.1.

TABLE 1.1
District-wise Distribution of Units Comprising the Universe and the Sample

Sr. No.	Districts	District-wise distribution of units comprising the universe	Proposed district-wise distribution of sample units	Effective district-wise distribution of sample units
1	2	3	4	5
1.	Ambala	2157	50	47
2.	Bhiwani	890	20	19
3.	Faridabad	2313	52	50
4.	Gurgaon	1299	30	28
5.	Hissar	1411	33	31
6.	Jind	1074	25	23
7.	Karnal	2610	58	56
8.	Kurukshetra	701	16	15
9.	Mahendergarh	900	20	19
10.	Rohtak	2166	49	47
11.	Sirsa	722	17	16
12.	Sonepat	1321	30	29
	Total	17564	400	380

Source : Small-scale Industries Directory of Haryana, 1981-82.

Questionnaires got filled up from 20 units were discarded during the course of editing because of their being incomplete or inconsistent, thus leaving an effective sample of 380 units with district-wise distribution as given in the Col. (5) of the table.

The analysis is finally based on data on each aspect/ characteristic tabulated both according to the various size-groups and different product-groups. Besides making use of simple descriptive tools of statistics such as mean, percentages, and ranks, possible relationships have been brought out through cross-sectional analysis. Wherever necessary and feasible, these relationships have been highlighted by computing the coefficient of correlation. In the analysis of responses involving ranking, ranks have been converted into scores by assigning a weightage of 4 to the first rank, of 3 to the second rank, and so on, to obtain total scores or the overall ranking order based thereon.

Thus, the whole analysis is carried out in eight chapters. Besides the first chapter on Introduction, chapter II gives a detailed description of the profile of the sample units in respect of form of organisation, asset-size, nature of product produced, age, size of employment, etc. The next four chapters, III to VI, bring out the marketing practices in relation to product, price, promotion, and distribution, respectively. While chapter VII is devoted to highlighting policies and practices on sales forecasting, geographical coverage, credit facilities, inventories, and the relative importance of the four elements of marketing mix, the last chapter puts together the main points emerging from the preceding analysis as 'findings'.

Chapter II

Sample Units : A Profile

In this chapter we shall bring out some of the important characteristics of the sample units insofar as they may have a direct or indirect bearing on their choice of marketing policies and practices. These characteristics relate to the form of organization, asset size, nature of the product-groups, age of the units, size of employment, and investment. Accordingly, the analysis is based on the distribution of sample units according to the forms of organization, asset size-groups, product-groups, and age-groups.

2.1 FORM OF ORGANIZATION AND ASSET SIZE-GROUPS

Table 2.1 gives the classification of sample units of various size-groups according to the forms of organization, viz., sole-proprietorship, partnership, joint-stock company and 'others'. It reveals the following:

i) Out of 380 sample units, about 45 per cent are being run on sole-proprietorship basis and 41 per cent are partnership firms. Only a limited number, comprising 8 per cent, are joint-stock companies. According to the three groupings based on asset size, 52.6 per cent are of small size, 36.3 per cent of medium size, and 11.1 per cent of large size.

ii) Out of those belonging to the small-size group, 60.0 per cent are being run on sole-proprietorship basis, 30.0 per cent on partnership basis, and only 2.0 per cent as joint-stock companies. The medium size-group is different inasmuch as 58 per cent of these are run on partnership basis and 30.4 per cent on sole-proprietorship basis. The proportion of joint-stock companies here increases to 8.7 per cent.

TABLE 2.1

Distribution of Sample Units of Various Size-groups According to the Forms of Organization

Forms of organization	Size-groups			
	Small	Medium	Large	Total
1	2	3	4	5
Sole-proprietorship	120	42	8	170
	(60.0)	(30.4)	(19.)	(44.7)
Partnership	60	80	16	156
	(30.0)	(58.0)	(38.1)	(41.1)
Joint-stock company	4	12	16	32
	(2.0)	(8.7)	38.1)	(8.4)
Others*	16	4	2	22
	(8.0)	(2.9)	(4.8)	(5.8)
Total	200	138	42	380
	(52.6)	(36.3)	(11.0)	(100.0)

(Figures in parentheses under Cols. 3 to 5 are percentages to their respective totals in the last row, and those in the last row and last column are percentages to all the 380 units comprising the sample.)

* Such as Gram Udyog Mandal, Joint Hindu Family, etc.

iii) In the case of large size-group, 38.1 per cent are run on partnership basis and an equal proportion consists of joint-stock companies. Sole-proprietorship firms are only 19 per cent of the large units.

From the above it follows that while the largest proportion of small-scale units are being run on sole-proprietorship basis, followed closely by those of partnership firms and, with a wide margin, the joint-stock companies. Sole-proprietorship form of organization is most common in the case of units belonging to the small size-group, whereas the medium size group is dominated by the partnership form of organization. In the case of large size-group, partnership firms and joint–stock companies have equal preponderance. It is important, though obvious, to note at the overall level that the number of units falling in the various size-groups tends to decrease with the increase in asset size. This also holds good in the case of sole-proprietorship firms as well as those run on partnership basis. Contrary to this, the number of joint-stock companies increases with the increase in asset size. The behaviour of the number of units belonging to the various forms of organization is also not altogether unexpected. That is, the number of sample units tends to decrease as we move from sole-proprietorship to partnership, and from partnership to joint-stock companies. This is applicable at the overall level as also to the three size-groups separately.

Interestingly, there exists a positive association between asset size and the form of organization. The cross-classified data presented in Table 2.1, which permits the use of Chi-square Test of Independence, proves it to be so. The computed value of the capital chi-square notation (χ^2) comes to $\chi^2 = 91.0$ which is much greater than the tabulated χ^2 value $\chi^2_{.05} = 9.488$ at 5 per cent level of significance with degrees of freedom $\upsilon = 6$. This shows that the hypothesis of positive association between asset size and the form of organization is accepted. The correlation coefficient (r) based on the computed χ^2 value is

$$r = \sqrt{\frac{\chi^2}{n\,(K-1)}} = \sqrt{\frac{91.0}{380(4-1)}} = 0.28$$

which further shows that the association is positive.

2.2 FORM OF ORGANIZATION AND PRODUCT-GROUPS

When the form of organization is seen in relation to different product-groups, we come across some interesting results. Table 2.2, which gives the classification of sample units of different product-groups according to the forms of organization, shows the following:

TABLE 2.2

Distribution of Sample Units of Different Product-groups According to the Form of Organization

Forms of organization	Product-groups				
	Chemicals	Textiles	Engineering	Metals	Food-Wood
1	2	3	4	5	6
Sole-proprietorship	30 (42.9)	18 (33.3)	56 (51.9)	38 (42.2)	28 (48.3)
Partnership	34 (48.6)	28 (51.9)	36 (33.3)	34 (37.8)	24 (41.4)
Joint-stock companies	6 (8.5)	8 (14.8)	12 (11.1)	4 (4.4)	2 (3.4)
Others	0 (0.0)	0 (0.0)	4 (3.7)	14 (15.6)	4 (6.9)
Total	70 (18.4)	54 (14.2)	108 (28.4)	90 (23.7)	58 (15.3)

(Figures in parentheses under Cols. 3 to 7 are percentages to their respective totals in the last row, while those in the last row are percentages to the total number of units in the sample.)

i) The units selected in the sample are so distributed among different product-groups that 28 per cent of them belongs to engineering, 23.7 per cent to metals, 18.4 per cent to chemicals, 14 per cent to textiles, and the remaining 15.3 per cent to food-wood.

ii) Out of 170 units which are run on sole-proprietorship basis, the largest proportion belongs to engineering, followed, in a descending order, by those belonging to food-wood, chemicals, metals, and textiles. In the case of 156 units run on partnership basis, the maximum proportion of them belongs to Textiles, followed by Chemicals, Food-Wood, Metals, and Engineering where the proportion of such units is the lowest. A maximum proporation of 32 joint-stock companies falls in the textile group, followed, in a descending order, by the engineering, chemicals, metals, and food-wood product-groups.

iii) In chemicals and textiles, the highest proportion is of partnership firms, followed by those run on sole-proprietorship basis. The proportion of joint-stock companies is the lowest in both these product-groups.

iv) The position in respect of engineering and metals is different to the extent that the proporation of sole-proprietorship firms is the highest. food-wood also conforms to the same pattern.

It follows from the above that partnership form of organization is the most popular in the case of chemicals and textiles. Sole-proprietorship is relatively more prevalent in the case of engineering, metals, and food-wood product-groups.

2.3 AGE OF SAMPLE UNITS

Table 2.3 gives the cross-classification of sample units according to the various size and age-groups. It shows that the maximum number of sample units at the overall level falls in the 6-10 years age-group, followed, in a descending order, by those belonging to '10-20 years', 'less than 6 years', and 'more than 20 years' age-groups. This pattern also holds for units falling in all the three asset size-groups.

TABLE 2.3

Distribution of Sample Units of Various Size-groups According to Age-groups

Age-groups	Size-groups			
	Small	Medium	Large	Total
1	2	3	4	5
Below 6 years	46 (23.0)	32 (23.2)	10 (23.8)	88 (23.1)

1	2	3	4	5
6-10	68	38	14	120
	(34.0)	(27.5)	(33.3)	(31.6)
10-20	62	38	12	112
	(31.0)	(27.5)	(28.6)	(29.5)
More than	24	30	6	60
20 years	(12.0)	(21.8)	(14.3)	(15.8)
Average age (yrs.)	9.21	12.23	9.0	10.3
Total	200	138	42	380
	(100.0)	(100.0)	(100.0)	(100.0)

(Figures in parentheses are percentages to their respective totals.)

The position emerging in different product-groups is not as neat as in terms of the various size-groups. Classification of sample units according to various age and product-groups, as in table 2.4, shows that the average age is the highest in the case of engineering units, followed, in a descending order, by those falling in metals, food-wood, textiles, and chemicals. Further, the engineering product-group has the maximum proportion of units belonging to '10-20 years' and 'more than 20 years' age-groups. Chemicals and textiles have the highest proportion of units falling in the age-group of 'less than 6 years', and metals and food-wood in age-group of '6-10 years'. The lowest proportion of units in the age groups of 'less than 6 years' and 10-20 years' belongs to metals, in '6-10 years' belongs to textiles, and in 'more than 20 years' belongs to textiles.

TABLE 2.4

Distribution of Sample Units of Different Product-groups According to Age-groups

Age-groups	Product-groups				
	Chemicals	Textiles	Engineering	Metals	Food-Wood
1	2	3	4	5	6
Below 6 years	22	20	16	12	18
	(31.4)	(37.1)	(14.8)	(13.3)	(31.0)
6-10	18	12	28	44	18
	(25.7)	(22.21)	(25.9)	(48.9)	(31.0)

1	2	3	4	5	6
10-20	20	18	40	20	14
	(28.6)	(33.3)	(37.1)	(22.2)	(24.2)
More than 20	10	4	24	14	8
years	(14.3)	(7.4)	(22.2)	(15.6)	(13.8)
Average age (yrs.)	7.5	8.7	13.0	10.8	9.1
Total	70	54	108	90	58
	(100.0)	(100.0)	(100.0)	(100.0)	(100.0)

(Figures in parentheses are percentages of the respective totals.)

It is not wholly without basis to expect a positive relationship between age and asset size. The reason being that in the normal course a firm would acquire more assets with a view to expanding its operations as the period during which it remains in business tends to increase. Table 2.5, which gives average asset size classified according to different age-groups and size-groups, effectively brings out this relationship. At the overall level the average asset size has increased from Rs. 9.2 lac in the lowest age-group of 'below 6 years' to Rs. 11.8 lac in the highest age-group of 'more than 20 years'. It increases from Rs. 3.3 lac in the lowest

TABLE 2.5

Average Asset Size According to Size-groups and Age-groups

Age-groups	Average Asset-size (Rs. lac)			
	Small	Medium	Large	Total
1	2	3	4	5
Below 6 years	3.3	11.1	28.9	9.2
6-10	2.8	11.3	21.5	7.0
10-20	4.9	11.0	22.0	9.8
More than 20 years	6.6	16.0	19.0	11.8
Overall average asset size	4.0	12.2	23.3	9.1

age-group to Rs. 6.6 lac in the highest age-group in the case of units belonging to the small size-group. In the case of medium size-group, the average asset-size has increased from Rs. 11.1 lac in the lowest age-group to Rs. 16.0 lac in the highest age-group. The positive relationship between age and asset-size is, however, not met in the case of units belonging to the large size-group, where the average asset-size has declined from Rs. 28.9 lac in the lowest age-group to Rs. 19.0 lac in the highest age-group.

2.4 CAPITAL INVESTED

As shown in Table 2.6, which presents the data on fixed capital, gross working capital, and the ratio of the fixed capital to the gross working capital according to the form of organization, the value of fixed capital is the lowest in units run on the sole-proprietorship basis, and the highest in joint-stock companies. Similar is the position in respect of gross working capital.

TABLE 2.6

Average Per Unit Gross Working Capital, Fixed Capital, and Ratio of Fixed Capital to Gross Working Capital According to Forms of Organization

Forms of organization	Fixed capital (Rs. lac)	Gross working capital (Rs. lac)	Ratio of fixed capital to gross working capital (Times)
1	2	3	4
Sole-poprietorship	4.47	2.05	2.18
Partnership	6.87	2.87	2.39
Joint-stock company	14.15	7.02	2.01
Others	5.01	2.00	2.50

The ratio of fixed capital to gross working capital, ignoring the category of 'others', is the highest in the case of partnership firms and the lowest in joint-stock companies. The lower this ratio is, the more convenient a firm should feel in terms of the availability of working capital. *Ceteris paribus*, it implies that a firm with a lower ratio of fixed capital to gross working capital should be able to spare more funds for marketing activities. When so viewed, the joint-stock companies are placed in a relatively better position. And this is what it ought to be, since firms of large size should be at ease in sparing funds for the marketing activities. Firms run on sole-proprietorship basis compare equally well with the joint-stock companies. Partnership firms, however, do appear to be in a relatively disadvantageous position in regard to their capacity to spare funds for marketing activities.

Table 2.7 gives the value of fixed capital, gross working capital, and ratio of fixed capital to gross working capital

TABLE 2.7

Average Per Unit Gross Working Capital, Fixed Capital, and Ratio of Fixed Capital to Gross Working Capital According to Different Product-groups

Product-groups	Fixed capital (Rs. lac)	Gross working (Rs. lac)	Ratio of fixed capital to gross (Times)
1	2	3	4
Chemicals	4.67	8.09	1.74
Textiles	2.36	9.32	3.94
Engineering	2.68	5.54	2.07
Metals	2.15	5.31	2.47
Food-Wood	2.23	4.68	2.11

according to various product-groups. It shows that the value of fixed capital is the highest in chemicals, followed, in a descending order, by engineering, textiles, food-wood and metals. The gross working capital is the highest in textiles, followed, in a descending order and with a wide margin, by chemicals, engineering, metals, and food-wood where it is the minimum. The ratio of fixed capital to gross working capital is the highest in textiles and the lowest in chemicals. This means that the chemical product group is placed in the most convenient position insofar as it appears to have the maximum capacity to spare funds for marketing. Engineering and food-wood product-groups are also placed in a better position as compared to metals and textiles.

The ratios of fixed capital to gross working capital as given in Table 2.8, classified according to various product-groups and size-groups, further show that this ratio is minimum in chemicals and the highest in textiles in all the size-groups. A high ratio of fixed capital to gross working capital indicates that long-term funds for developing markets are available in a larger quantum with the textile units. The relative positioning of the various product-groups is identical in the case of medium and large-size groups. The small size-group presents a slightly different picture to the extent that the ratio of fixed capital to gross working capital is relatively lower in metals as compared to engineering as against a reverse position obtaining in the medium and large size-groups. An important pattern which has emerged is that this ratio increases with the increase in asset size in the case of all the product-groups.

TABLE 2.8

Ratios of Fixed Capital to Gross Working Capital According to Different Product-groups and Size-groups

Product-groups	Size-groups		
	Small	Medium	Large
1	2	3	4
Chemicals	2.38	2.46	2.77
Textiles	3.23	4.72	5.75
Engineering	3.12	3.14	3.51
Metals	2.62	3.56	4.17
Food-wood	3.18	3.61	5.36

2.5 SIZE OF EMPLOYMENT

The classification of sample units according to the size of employment yields some important results. Table 2.9, which gives such classification, brings out that about 38 per cent of the sample units employ 'more than 10 but less than 20' persons, while 33 per cent of them employ 'less than 10'

TABLE 2.9

Distribution of Sample Units According to Size of Employment Per Unit

Number of employees per unit	Number of units	Per cent to total	Cumulative totals	Per cent cumulative total
1	2	3	4	5
Less than 10	126	33.1	126	33.1
10 to 20	144	37.9	270	71.0
20 to 30	54	14.2	324	85.2
30 to 50	36	9.6	360	94.7
50 to 100	14	3.7	374	98.4
More than 100	6	1.6	380	100.0
Total	380	100.0		

persons. Interestingly, there are only 13 per cent of the sample units which provide employment to persons ranging 'between 30 to 100'. On the whole, there are about 71 per cent of the units which employ 'less than 20' persons. This percentage increases to 85 for units employing 'less than 30' persons, which by itself is a significant result.

According to Table 2.10 which gives the size of employment and the capital invested according to various size-groups, on an average each unit offers employment to 18 persons. The position in terms of the various size-groups is quite consistent insofar as the average number of persons employed is the lowest in the small size-group, followed, with a wide margin, by the medium and large size-groups. Capital invested per person follows the same pattern. It is the lowest in the small size-group, followed in an ascending order, by the medium and large size-groups. This implies that smaller units offer much greater employment potential with much lower investment as compared to units of medium and large size.

TABLE 2.10

Size of Employment and Capital Invested Per Person According to Various Size-groups

Size-groups	Number of units	Average number of persons employed in each unit	Capital per person (Rs. '000)
1	2	3	4
Small	200	11	4.8
Medium	138	20	17.8
Large	42	47	21.6
Total	380	18	14.8

Table 2.11 gives the average number of employees and capital invested per person according to various product-groups. It shows that the textiles product-group is most employment oriented as each unit in this group offers employment, on an average, to as many as 35 persons. Interestingly, it is again the textile product-group in which most of the units are of small size. This is followed, in a

TABLE 2.11

Size of Employment and Capital Invested Per Person According to Different Product-groups

Product-groups	Number of units	Average number of persons employed in each unit	Capital invested per person (Rs. '000)
1	2	3	4
Chemicals	70	17	20.0
Textiles	54	35	14.1
Engineering	108	19	11.7
Metals	90	14	14.9
Food-Wood	58	10	16.8
Total	380	18	14.8

descending order and with a wide margin, by the engineering and chemicals, where the average number of persons employed are 19 and 17, respectively. The average number of employees is about 14 in metals and 10 in food-wood. As against this, capital invested per person is the highest in chemicals, followed, in a descending order, by food-wood, metals, textiles, and engineering.

Chapter III

Product Planning and Development

Product occupies a unique place in the marketing mix of a firm. So important is the role of product that all decisions involving the other elements of marketing mix, viz., pricing, promotion, and distribution, are taken in relation to product. How well a product sells in the market is one of the basic criteria of judging the performance of a firm. Since a product is essentially a source of need satisfaction, every producer has to ensure that his offer to the customers is as best as possible. It should be the best not only as a *core product,* but also as a *formal product* which is a *larger package* referring to all such characteristics as quality, design, style, brand name, and packaging. When a product is viewed in this broader sense, the role of product planning becomes a lot more significant in formulating an appropriate marketing strategy.

The manner how a product is developed and finally offered for sale to the customers are the two basic issues that go into the formulation of product planning with its focus on winning over customers' affiliation and achieving greater market penetration. The scope of product planning becomes much wider and complex in situations where a firm is engaged in the production and marketing of a number of items belonging to one or more related products. Under these circumstances product planning is more concerned with deciding an appropriate *product-mix.*

Here we shall bring out and analyse the general practices

that are being followed by the small-scale units in respect of some important aspects of product planning such as product-mix, product development, product standardization, branding, and packaging. The emphasis is on identifying the similarities and differences in terms of various size-groups and product-groups.

3.1 PRODUCT MIX

Frequently we come across firms, whether engaged in manufacturing, wholesaling, or retailing, which deal with more than one product. A product may have different items distinguishable in terms of price, size, appearance, or some other attribute. These may belong to one or more product line(s). A product line is defined as a group of product items which are related either because they satisfy similar needs of different market segments, or different but related needs of a given market segment.

A product mix is a set of all product lines and items that a particular seller offers for sale. The product mix of a firm may be described in terms of having a certain width and depth. The width of the product mix refers to the number of product lines handled by a firm. The depth of the product mix, on the other hand, indicates the average number of items in each product line. It is possible to obtain the average of the depth of different lines of a firm to use it as a measure of the typical depth of its product mix. The depth of the product mix here used for purposes of analysis has been obtained accordingly. The depth of the product mix is said to be too short if addition of an item or more is likely to yield higher profit. Contrary to this, the depth of the mix is considered to be too long if dropping of one or more items from the line results in increased profits. The question of optimality of the depth of the product mix, however, depends, to a large extent, on the objectives a firm may try to achieve.

While the limitations of data do not permit us to go into the question whether the depth of the product-mix is too long or too short, it is possible to bring out the position in respect of the average number of items handled by each firm, the width and depth of the product-mix, and gross profit in terms of the various size-groups and product-groups. Table 3.1, which gives the position on product mix and

TABLE 3.1

Product Mix and Gross Profit Rate According to Various Size-groups

Size-groups	Average number of items per unit	Width of product mix	Depth of product mix	Average gross profit (as % to sales) rate per unit
1	2	3	4	5
Small	4.2	2.2	1.9	16.9
Medium	4.7	2.1	2.2	14.8
Large	2.1	1.3	1.6	14.3

gross profit rate according to various size-groups, shows that the average number of items produced per unit is the smallest (2.1) in the case of units belonging to the large size-group. It is double in the small and, even more, in the medium size-group. On an average, the width of the product mix in the large size-group is almost half of the width in the other two, small and medium, size-groups. That is, in general the units belonging to the medium and small size-groups pursue two product lines as against one in the large size-group. The relative position of the three size-groups indicates that as a manufacturing unit tends to expand in terms of the size of its assets, it prefers to specialize in the production of a limited number of lines.

The depth of product mix is the lowest (1.6) in the large size-group and the highest (2.2) in the medium size-group. The small size-group is closer to the medium than to the large size-group. In other words, the relativity among the three size-groups in respect of the depth of the product mix is almost the same as obtained in the case of average number of items produced per unit.

The relative position of the three size-groups with regard to average gross profit rate is identical to that of the width of the product mix. The gross profit rate is the highest (16.9%) in the case of small size-group, 14.8 per cent in the medium size-group, and the lowest (14.3%) in the large size-group. Significantly, the gross profit rate tends to decline with the increase in asset size. It goes counter to the generally held view that smaller units are less profitable as compared to large units.

The position in respect of different product-groups, based on Table 3.2, is as under:

(i) The average number of items produced per unit is the maximum (5.1) in metals and the lowest (2.8) in food-wood. It is 3.5 in textiles and 4.3 each in chemicals and engineering.

(ii) The width of the product mix is again maximum (2.7) in metals and the lowest (1.1) in food-wood. It is 2.2 in engineering and 1.9 each in chemicals and textiles.

TABLE 3.2

Product Mix and Gross Profit Rate
According to different Product-groups

Product-groups	Average number of items per unit	Width of product mix	Depth of product mix	Average gross-profit (as % to sales) rate per unit
1	2	3	4	5
Chemicals	4.3	1.9	2.3	14.1
Textiles	3.5	1.9	1.8	12.6
Engineering	4.3	2.2	1.9	15.3
Metals	5.1	2.7	1.9	13.6
Food-wood	2.8	1.1	2.5	16.2

(iii) The picture obtaining in terms of the depth of the product mix is much different as it is the maximum (2.5) in food-wood, followed very closely by chemicals (2.3). Although the depth is the lowest (1.8) in textiles, it is not much different from that in engineering and metals (1.9).

(iv) The relative position of the various product-groups in terms of the gross profit rate is closer to that obtained in respect of the depth of the product-mix. The gross profit rate is the highest (16.2%) in food-wood and the lowest (12.6%) in textiles. Engineering and chemical product-groups are also placed in a comfortable position with gross profit rate at 15.3 per cent and 14.1 per cent, respectively. Here a positive relationship between the depth of product mix and gross profit rate is discernible.

3.2 PRODUCT DEVELOPMENT

Product development is an important marketing activity. The success of a product in the market depends mainly on whether or not the product has been developed in keeping with the needs of its customers. No firm can hope to survive in the market for long unless it adopts product development as a continuous process. In a wider sense, product development in its various dimensions, among other things, may consist of developing a new product, adding new item(s) to the existing product line, replacing an old item with a new one, and modifying an old product item.

In the present age of cut-throat competition and changing production techniques, product development in any of these ways may be based on developing own samples, modifying competitor's product, consulting technical experts, and conducting market surveys. It would be interesting to find out which of these techniques is more popular in the small-scale industries. Sample responses obtained in this regard have been presented according to various size-groups and product-groups in Table 3.3 and 3.4, respectively.

A persual of Table 3.3 shows that at the overall level only 54.7 per cent of the sample units are engaged in product development activity. While about 13.7 per cent of them make use of more than one technique of product development, 18.4 per cent resort to modifying competitor's product and 17.9 per cent develop their own samples. The use of the services of technical experts and market surveys is very limited.

Product development based on modifying competitor's product is the most popular in the case of small size group,

TABLE 3.3

Distribution of Sample Units of Various Size-groups According to the Techniques Used for Product Development

Product development techniques	Size-groups			
	Small	Medium	Large	Total
1	2	3	4	5
Developing own samples/ models	30 (15.0)	32 (23.2)	6 (14.3)	68 (17.9)
Modifying competitor's product	42 (21.0)	24 (17.4)	4 (9.5)	70 (18.4)
Consulting technical experts	4 (2.0)	4 (2.9)	6 (14.3)	14 (3.7)
Conducting market surveys	0 (0.0)	2 (1.4)	2 (4.7)	4 (1.0)
Those using more than one technique	24 (12.0)	16 (11.6)	12 (28.6)	52 (13.7)
Those with no product development activity	100 (50.0)	60 (43.5)	12 (28.6)	172 (45.3)
Total	200 (100.0)	138 (100.0)	42 (100.0)	380 (100.0)

(Figures in paretheses are percentages the respective totals in the last row.)

followed by developing own samples. While the market survey

approach is not at all used in this size-group, obtaining the advice of technical experts for developing new product is limited to two units only. The position in respect of the medium and large size-groups is different insofar as the technique of developing own samples is more frequently used in their case than that of modifying competitor's product. The use of the other two techniques, though limited, is relatively more in the medium and large size-groups as compared to the small size-group. Consultation with technical experts in the large size-group is, in fact, as popular as the technique of developing own samples. The proportion of units using the market survey approach is about 5 per cent in the large size-group as against 1 per cent in the medium size-group. About 12 per cent of the units each in the small and medium size-groups use more than one technique of product development as against about 29 per cent of the units in the large size-group.

An interesting pattern which has emerged is that the proportion of units not engaged in any product development activity has sharply declined with the increase in asset size. On the other hand, there is a visible tendency for increased use of more than one technique of product development as we move to units belonging to the large size-group. Although developing own samples and modifying competitor's product are the two most popular product development activities at the overall level and in the three size-groups independently, technical advice and market survey approaches are more frequently used in the large size-group. This is quite understandable, indeed.

The relative position of different product development techniques among different product-groups is broadly the same as obtained in terms of the various size-groups. Except in the case of engineering, where modifying competitor's product is most popular, developing own samples is most frequently used in all the remaining product-groups. Among these product-groups, developing own samples is the most

TABLE 3.4

Distribution of Sample Units of Different Product-groups According to the Techniques Used for Product Development

Product development techniques	Product-groups				
	Chemicals	Textiles	Engineering	Metals	Food-Wood
1	2	3	4	5	6
Developing own samples/models	14 (20.0)	14 (25.9)	14 (13.0)	20 (22.2)	6 (10.3)
Modifying competitor's product	12 (17.1)	10 (18.5)	28 (25.9)	16 (17.8)	4 (6.9)
Consulting technical experts	8 (11.4)	0 (0.0)	2 (1.85)	4 (4.5)	0 (0.0)
Conducting market surveys	2 (2.9)	0 (0.0)	2 (1.8)	0 (0.0)	0 (0.0)
Those using more than one technique	22 (31.4)	14 (25.9)	6 (5.6)	10 (11.1)	0 (0.0)
Those with no product development activity	12 (17.2)	16 (29.7)	56 (51.9)	40 (44.4)	48 (82.8)
Total	70 (100.0)	54 (100.0)	108 (100.0)	90 (100.0)	58 (100.0)

(Figures in parentheses are percentages of the respective totals in the last row.)

popular basis of product development in the case of textiles, followed closely by metals, chemicals, and, with a wide margin, engineering and food-wood. Modifying competitor's product is used by the highest proportion of units in engineering, followed closely by textiles, metals, chemicals, and food-wood. The advice of technical experts is most frequently used in chemicals and, with a significant gap, metals. The services of technical experts are not used at all in the remaining product-groups. Market surveys are conducted only by a limited number of units belonging to chemicals and engineering.

No efforts are made at product development in about 83 per cent of the food-wood units, 52 per cent of the engineering units, and about 44 per cent of the metal units. In chemicals and textiles the proportion of units not engaged in product development is 17.2 per cent and 29.7 per cent, respectively. There is a greater consciousness about product development in chemicals and textiles where about 31 per cent and 26 per cent of the units, respectively, have been found using multiple techniques of product development. The position of chemicals is unique where the use of the advice of technical experts is the maximum and the proportion of units not engaged in any product development activity is the lowest.

3.3 PRODUCT STANDARDIZATION

Among several factors which influence the marketability of a product, the quality aspect is of paramount importance in determining customers' faith in the adequacy of the product in satisfying their needs. Product quality is expressed through standardization of its inherent characteristics to meet the users' needs. As an assurance of the product being of desired quality, it must bear an appropriate ISI (Indian Standards Institute) mark. The use of ISI quality mark serves as a measure of product standardization which is an effective instrument of sales promotion. The position regarding the use of ISI quality mark both in terms of the various size-groups and product-groups reveals some interesting points.

Table 3.5, which brings out the use of quality mark according to the various size-groups, shows that as many as 55 per cent of the units belonging to the small size-group do not use any quality mark. While 40 per cent of them use their own mark, the use of ISI quality mark is limited only to the remaining 5 per cent of the sample units. The position improves in the case of units belonging to medium and large size-groups. While the proportion of units not using quality mark is 27.5 per cent in the medium-size group, it is just

19.1 per cent in the case of large size-group. The proportion of those using their own quality mark is 59.4 per cent in the medium-size group and 61.9 per cent in the large-size group. The ISI mark is used by 13.1 per cent of the units belonging to the medium size-group and about 19.1 per cent of those belonging to the large size-group. At the overall level, 41 per cent of the sample units use no quality mark and 49.5 per cent use their own quality mark. The proportion of those selling their products under ISI mark is just 9.5 per cent.

TABLE 3.5

Distribution of Sample Units of Various Size-groups According to the Type of Quality Mark Used

Size-groups	Sample units	Users of ISI mark	Users of own quality mark	Those using no quality mark
1	2	3	4	5
Small	200	10 (5.0)	80 (40.0)	110 (55.0)
Medium	138	18 (13.1)	82 (59.4)	38 (27.5)
Large	42	8 (19.1)	26 (61.9)	8 (19.1)
Total	380	36 (9.5)	188 (49.5)	156 (41.0)

(Figures in parentheses are percentages of the respective totals.)

The position above is indicative of a positive relationship between asset-size and the degree of product standardization achieved insofar as it is expressed through the use of ISI mark. That is, there is a greater consciousness for quality improvement and adoption of definite quality mark as the scale of operations increases. The fact, however, remains that a large number of small-scale units have not adopted any quality mark for their products. This is particularly so in the case of units of small size where the proportion of units using no quality mark is as high as 55 per cent. Interestingly, the trend to make use of own quality mark has not weakened even with the increase in asset size. The proportion of units using own quality mark, which is the lowest in the small size-group and the highest in the large size-group, has been higher than the proportion of those using ISI mark in all the size-groups.

The position in respect of the various product-groups is as given in Table 3.6. It is interesting to note that the proportion of units using no quality mark is the highest (55.6%) in textiles, followed, in a descending order, by food-wood, engineering, metals and, with a wide margin, chemicals. As against this, the proportion of units using their own mark is as high as 68.6 per cent in chemicals, 57.8 per cent in metals, and about 40 per cent in each of the remaining three product-groups. ISI quality mark is used most frequently in engineering, followed by food-wood and chemicals. Its use is too limited in textiles and metals.

TABLE 3.6

Distribution of Sample Units of Different Product-groups According to the Type of Quality Mark Used

Product-groups	Sample units	Use of ISI mark	Users of own quality mark	Those using no quality mark
1	2	3	4	5
Chemicals	70	6 (8.6)	48 (68.6)	16 (22.8)
Textiles	54	2 (3.7)	22 (40.7)	30 (55.6)
Engineering	108	18 (16.7)	42 (38.9)	48 (44.4)
Metals	90	4 (4.4)	52 (57.8)	34 (37.8)

1	2	3	4	5
Food-wood	58	6 (10.3)	24 (41.4)	28 (48.3)
Total	380	36 (9.5)	188 (49.5)	156 (41.0)

(Figures in parentheses are percentages to their respective totals.)

While the proportion of units using ISI quality mark is much less as compared to those using their own quality mark in the case of all the product-groups, it is only in the case of chemicals and metals that the proportion of units using no quality mark is much less than that of those using their own quality mark. On the whole, the chemical product-group is far ahead in product standardization than the other product-groups. The position is also satisfactory in metals and engineering, with textiles trailing far behind.

3.4 BRANDING

Branding is the act of giving a specific name, term, sign, symbol, design, or a combination of these, to a product by its producer or seller. The basic purpose of branding is to create uniqueness in the product, since it helps identify the product produced/sold by a producer/seller or a group of them, and to differentiate it from those of its rival(s). When a brand has been granted legal protection in the sense that it cannot be used by any one else, such a brand is called a *trade mark*. A registered brand-holder undertakes the guarantee to maintain quality standards of the product, and make it known to customers through advertisement. In all, the basic function of branding is to help the customers identify the product and its producers or sellers and provide them with an opportunity to earn goodwill and repeat patronage.

There are several choices available to producer(s) giving brand name to their products. Under one of these choices a manufacturer or seller may sell his product under his own brand name. When one does this, it is called manufacturer's or seller's brand. Alternatively, a producer may allow the middlemen to sell his product under their own brand name. This is known as private brand. Where products lack common marketing attributes, each of them ean be given independent brand name and sold as such. This is known as individual brand. Individual branding is generally used when product items are not similar in quality, product line is not compatible, and the products are not sold in the same market. On the other hand, a producer may go in for family branding where a single brand name is used for all the products marketed by the same producer or seller.

To bring out the position regarding various issues relating to branding, we may refer to the data presented according to various size-groups in Table 3.7, and according to different

TABLE 3.7

Distribution of Sample Units of Various Size-groups According to Brand Use Characteristics

Size-groups	Sample units	Brand name users	Brand name non-users	Type of brand: Individual brand users	Type of brand: Family brand users	Whether registered brand or unregistered: Registered	Whether registered brand or unregistered: Unregistered
1	2	3	4	5	6	7	8
Small	200	92 (46.0)	108 (54.0)	8 (8.7)	84 (91.3)	46 (50.0)	46 (50.0)
Medium	138	74 (53.6)	64 (46.4)	8 (10.8)	66 (89.2)	54 (72.9)	20 (27.0)
Large	42	26 (61.9)	16 (38.1)	0 (0.0)	26 (100.0)	14 (53.9)	12 (46.2)
Total	380	192 (50.5)	188 (49.5)	16 (8.3)	176 (91.7)	114 (59.4)	78 (40.6)

(Figures in parentheses are percentages.)

product-groups in Table 3.8. A persual of Table 3.7 shows that while the proportion of units not using any brand name is greater than that of those using it in the case of small size-group, it is the reverse that obtains in the case of medium and large size-groups. And it is significant that the proportion of units using brand name tends to increase with the increase in asset size. Among the brand users (192), the proportion of units using family brand is much more than that of individual brand users in all the three size-groups. It may be attributed to the fact that the average number of product lines per unit declines with the increase in the asset size of the unit. The use of registered brands is more popular than that of unregistered brands in all the three size-groups, particularly more so in the case of medium size-group.

Table 3.8, which gives the position in respect of different product-groups, shows that the proportion of brand users is the highest in chemicals, followed, with a wide margin,

TABLE 3.8

Distribution of Sample Units of Different Product-groups According to Brand Use Characteristics

Size-groups	Sample units	Brand name users	Brand name non-users	Type of brand		Whether registered brand or unregistered	
				Individual brand users	Family brand users	Registered	Unregistered
1	2	3	4	5	6	7	8
Chemicals	70	58 (82.9)	12 (17.1)	10 (17.2)	48 (82.8)	40 (69.0)	18 (31.0)
Textiles	54	20 (37.0)	34 (63.0)	2 (10.0)	18 (90.0)	4 (20.0)	16 (80.0)
Engineering	108	58 (53.7)	30 (46.3)	4 (6.9)	54 (93.1)	32 (55.2)	26 (44.8)
Metals	90	26 (28.9)	62 (71.1)	0 (0.0)	26 (100.0)	18 (69.2)	8 (30.8)

1	2	3	4	5	6	7	8
Food-wood	58	30 (51.7)	28 (48.3)	0 (0.0)	30 (100.0)	20 (66.7)	10 (33.3)
Total	380	192 (50.5)	188 (49.5)	16 (8.3)	176 (91.7)	114 (59.4)	78 (40.6)

(Figures in parentheses are percentages.)

by engineering, food-wood, textiles and metals. The proportion of brand users is much higher than that of the non-users in the case of chemicals and, with a much less difference, engineering, and food-wood. It is the reverse that obtains in the case of textiles and metals.

As regards the use of two (family and individual) branding policies, family branding is more popular than individual branding in àll the product-groups. In food-wood and metal product-groups the use of individual branding is completely absent. It is used by 17.2 per cent of the units in chemicals, 10 per cent in textiles, and just 6.9 per cent in engineering. While the proportion of units using unregistered brand is the maximum in textiles (80%), it is much less in all the remaining product-groups with the lowest (30.8%) in metals. As against this, the proportion of users of registered brand is the highest (69.2%) in metals, followed very closely by chemicals, food-wood, engineering, and textiles where it is the lowest (20%).

On the whole, it may be observed that the use of branding is more popular in the medium and large size-groups than in the small size-group. This is particularly so in the case of units belonging to chemicals, engineering and food-wood. That the frequency of family brand users is much higher than that of individual brand users in all the size-groups holds goods according to all the product-groups as well. Registered brands are more popular in all the size-groups, as also in the various product-groups except textiles.

3.5 PACKAGING

Products must be properly packed before they are sold to

the ultimate buyers. Packing is a physical activity which adds to convenience in handling the products and prevents leakages, flow-outs, or pilferages. The scope of packaging is much wider than that of packing. The former is regarded as a much more important marketing activity because it is used by the producers or sellers as a means of explanation, assurance, encouragement, and confidence — all directed to product buyers/customers. For the customers it is an effective means of recognizing the product and differentiating its characteristics from those of its rival products. It helps establish customer preferences for the product which ensure repeat purchases. A package which is attractive in design with good looking wrapper round the container always acts as an effective medium of advertising. Apart from giving necessary information to the buyers, it encourages them to do impulsive buying. Thus, it is primarily due to these and various other useful functions that producers and sellers spend large sums of money on packaging. It would, therefore, be revealing to bring out the importance of packaging as a marketing activity.

Table 3.9 gives, according to various size-groups, the expenditure on packaging, the proportion of sample units which consider packaging as an important marketing activity, and that of those which do not. It is interesting to note that

TABLE 3.9

Distribution of Sample Units of Various Size-groups According to Packaging Expenses and Importance of Packaging as a Marketing Activity

Size-groups	Sample units	Average packaging expenses (Rs. '000)	Units which consider packaging important	Units which do not consider packaging important
1	2	3	4	5
Small	200	15.4	72 (36.0)	128 (64.0)

1	2	3	4	5
Medium	138	110.8	102 (73.9)	36 (26.1)
Large	42	63.8	32 (76.2)	10 (23.8)
Total	380	55.3	206 (54.2)	174 (45.8)

(Figures in parantheses are percentages of total sample units in the respective size-groups.)

average expenditure on packaging is the lowest in the case of units belonging to the small size-group and the highest in the case of those belonging to the medium size-group. Average packaging expenses incurred by units of large size-group is almost half of that in the case of medium size-group. Most of the units in the case of large (76.2%) and medium (73.9%) size-group consider packaging as an important marketing activity. Only one third of the units (36%) in the small size-group deems it as a significant marketing activity. An important relationship which follows from the above is that the use of packaging increases with the increase in the asset size of the firms.

Table 3.10, which gives the position according to different product-groups, shows that the average expenses on

TABLE 3.10

Distribution of Sample Units of Different Product-groups According to Packaging Expenses and Importance of Packaging as a Marketing Activity

Size-groups	Sample units	Average packaging expenses (Rs.'000)	Units which consider packaging important	Units which do not consider packaging important
1	2	3	4	5
Chemicals	70	192.8	68 (97.1)	2 (2.9)

1	2	3	4	5
Textiles	54	24.8	32 (59.3)	22 (40.7)
Engineering	108	32.8	40 (37.0)	68 (63.0)
Metals	90	9.8	28 (31.1)	62 (68.9)
Food-wood	58	30.8	38 (65.5)	20 (34.5)
Total	380	55.3	206 (54.2)	174 (45.8)

(Figures in parentheses are percentages of total sample units in the respective product-groups.)

packaging is the highest in chemicals, followed, with a wide margin, by engineering, food-wood, and textiles, the lowest being in metals. Packaging is considered an important marketing activity by 97.1 per cent of the units in the chemical group. Food-wood comes next with 65.5 per cent of the units making such a claim, followed closely by textiles (59.3%). It is relatively less important in engineering, and the least in metals.

3.5.1 OBJECTIVES OF PACKAGING

The distribution of sample units of various size-groups according to different objectives of packaging, as given in Table 3.11, shows that convenience in handling is considered to be the basic packaging objective by the highest proportion of units belonging to all the size-groups, followed, in a descending order, by the objectives of product protection, and sales by description. Attracting customers is the least important objective of packaging in all the units irrespective of size. As between the various size-groups, convenience in handling is the most popular consideration in the medium size-group and the least popular in the large size-group. The objective of product protection is the most popular among the units of small size and the least popular among those of medium size. Sales by description is the most popular objective for units of large size and the least for those of small size. Similar is the position about packaging as a source of attracting customers which tends to become more popular with the increase in asset size of the firms.

TABLE 3.11

Distribution of Sample Units of Various Size-groups According to Objectives of Packaging

Packaging objectives	Size-groups			
	Small	Medium	Large	Total
1	2	3	4	5
Convenience in handling	40 (55.8)	60 (58.8)	10 (31.3)	110 (53.4)
Product protection	20 (27.8)	22 (21.6)	8 (25.0)	50 (24.3)
Sales by description	12 (16.7)	14 (13.7)	8 (25.0)	34 (16.5)
Attracting customers	0 (0.0)	6 (5.9)	6 (18.7)	12 (5.8)
Total	72 (100.0)	102 (100.0)	32 (100.0)	206 (100.0)

(Figures in parentheses are percentages of the respective column totals.)

The order of importance of various objectives of packaging among different product-groups is as shown in Table 3.12. It is revealing to find that convenience in handling is the most popular objective in all the product-groups, followed, in a descending order of importance, by the objectives of product protection, sales by description, and attracting customers. Among the various product-groups, convenience in handling is the most popular objective in metals, followed by engineering, and textiles. It is least popular in the case of food-wood. Product protection is the most popular in chemicals, followed by food-wood, textiles, engineering, and metals. Almost similar is the case in respect of the objective of sales by description. Attracting customers is not at all

TABLE 3.12

Distribution of Sample Units of different Product-groups According to Objectives of Packaging

Packaging objectives	Product-groups					
	Chemicals	Textiles	Engi-neering	Metals	Food-wood	Total
1	2	3	4	5	6	7
Convenience in handling	28 (41.2)	18 (56.3)	24 (60.0)	22 (78.6)	18 (47.4)	110 (53.4)
Product-protection	20 (29.4)	8 (25.0)	8 (20.0)	4 (14.4)	10 (26.3)	50 (24.3)
Sales by description	14 (20.6)	6 (18.7)	6 (15.0)	2 (7.0)	6 (15.8)	34 (16.5)
Attracting customers	6 (8.8)	0 (0.0)	2 (5.0)	0 (0.0)	4 (10.5)	12 (5.8)
Total	68 (100.0)	32 (100.0)	40 (100.0)	28 (100.0)	38 (100.0)	206 (100.0)

(Figures in parentheses are percentages of the respective column totals.)

popular in textiles and metals, while it does find some place in the remaining product-groups.

Chapter IV

Pricing Policies and Practices

What price is to be charged for a product is the most critical decision to be taken by the firm producing it. So important is the place of price in the the marketing mix of a firm that even when the product may have been matched with what suits the market, the actual transfer of its ownership takes place only after the buyers and the sellers have agreed on the price. Since price is the single element of marketing mix which produces revenue, it plays a distinctive role in determining the marketing success of a firm, irrespective of whether it is large or small. Although the non-price factors are receiving greater importance in terms of their role in the marketing success of a product, price is still viewed by many marketers as the most important element of marketing mix after the *product*. Product pricing has, therefore, to be handled with utmost care.

In the case of firms of large size, pricing decisions are taken by the production department in consultation with sales managers who have a direct feel of what may be accepted in the market. Pricing decisions in the case of small firms are taken by the top management which often includes the proprietors or the partners themselves. Since the small-scale units lack specialized field advice needed for price-setting, they follow pricing practices which are different from those followed by firms of large size in various ways. Here we shall dwell upon some important aspects of pricing, such as pricing objectives, factors influencing price setting, single pricing vis-a-vis multiple pricing, pricing in relation to competitors' prices, factors leading to change in prices, etc.

4.1 OBJECTIVES OF PRICING

Before setting the price of its product(s), a firm must be clear about the objective(s) it intends to achieve. This is necessary because each possible price will have different implications on profit, sales volume, and market share. Many firms set prices as would help maximize their profits. Such firms estimate the demand and costs associated with alternative prices and finally choose that price which offers maximum profit, cash inflow, or return on investment. Prices so determined are often incompatible with the social objectives. Alternatively, price-setting by a firm may be governed by the objective of achieving maximum growth in sales. It is often believed that this objective requires price setting at a relatively low level, although a low price may not necessarily result in a higher volume of sales.

The level at which the price of any product item (or product line) is fixed, may lead to reactions from the competitors. Fixing the price high would invite more competitors into the production of the concerned item(s). Pricing a product too low, on the other hand, may not always be possible without attracting adverse consequences, although, at times, it may even serve as a means to reduce competition. Therefore, meeting competition may be yet another objective of pricing. Some firms may be too keen to achieve a dominant market share. They are the ones which believe that a firm enjoying the largest market share will have the lowest costs and the highest long-term profit. Where this is the over-riding consideration, a firm may go in for capturing the larger market share by setting prices as low as possible.

The position of sample units belonging to various size-groups in terms of the average score obtained by different pricing objectives which they seek to achieve, is as given in Table 4.1. It shows that one of the sample units has adopted

TABLE 4.1*

Average Score Obtained by Different Pricing Objectives Under Various Size-groups

Objectives	Size-groups			
	Small	Medium	Large	Total
1	2	3	4	5
Target return on sales	1.8	1.9	2.1	1.9
Meeting competition	2.4	2.1	2.3	2.3
Sales growth	2.0	1.9	1.5	1.8
Increasing market share	0	0	0	0

*Here the responses were obtained in the form of ranks (1,2,3......., n). The ranks received by the various pricing objectives were converted into scores by assigning weights equal to (*n*, *n*-1, ..., 2, 1) and the average score computed for each size-group/product-group.

increase in market share as the pricing objective. Meeting competition has been the most important pricing objective at the overall level as also in the case of the three size-groups separately. While the objectives of target return on sales and sales growth have been equally popular for the units belonging to the medium size-group, the latter is the least popular in the case of large size-group and target return on sales in the case of small size-group.

Among the various size-groups, the objective of target return on sales is the most popular in the large size-group, followed by the medium and small size-groups. Meeting competition is the most popular in the small size-group and the least in the medium size-group. The objective of sales growth is the most common objective of pricing in the small size-group, followed by the medium and large size-groups. That is, sales growth tends to become less popular with the increase in the asset size.

Table 4.2, which gives the average score obtained by different pricing objectives under each product-group, shows that meeting competition is the most popular pricing

TABLE 4.2

Average Score Obtained by Various Pricing Objectives Under Different Product-groups

Objectives	Product-groups				
	Chemicals	Textiles	Engin-eering	Metals	Food-Wood
1	2	3	4	5	6
Target return on sales	1.7	2.2	1.8	1.7	1.8
Meeting competition	2.4	2.1	2.2	1.9	2.6
Sales growth	1.8	1.7	1.9	2.0	1.7
Increasing market share	0	0	0	0	0

(The average scores have been computed the same way as those in Table 4.1.)

objective in all the product-groups, except for textiles and metals. Target return on sales gets the first position in textiles, and sales growth in metals. While sales growth is the least important in textiles and food-wood, target return on sales holds a similar position in the case of chemicals and metals.

Across the various product-groups, the objective of target return on sales is the most popular in textiles, followed, in a descending order, by engineering and food-wood, and chemicals and metals. As regards the objective of meeting competition, it is the most popular in food-wood, followed, in a descending order, by chemicals, engineering, textiles, and metals. Sales growth is the most popular in metals, followed by engineering, chemicals, and food-wood and textiles.

4.2 FACTORS INFLUENCING PRICE-SETTING

The price at which a product is offered for sale in the market is affected by several factors both internal and external. Internal factors include interactions among the remaining three (product, distribution and promotion) marketing controllables and the cost. External factors include competitors' prices, buyer behaviour, overall economic climate, government policies, etc. Out of these, cost of production, product demand, competitors' prices, overall market conditions, and consumer paying capacity are some of the important factors which have a direct bearing on price-setting. The relative importance of each of these factors is brought out in Tables 4.3 and 4.4.

Table 4.3, which gives the distribution of total responses of the sample units of different size-groups according to the various factors influencing price setting, shows that cost of production is the most important factor which is kept in view while fixing prices. This is true of units belonging to all the size-groups As between the three size-groups, it

TABLE 4.3

Distribution of Total Responses of Sample Units of Various Size-groups According to Factors Influencing Price-setting

Factors	Size-groups			
	Small	Medium	Large	Total
1	2	3	4	5
Cost of production	168 (44.9)	128 (43.5)	38 (42.2)	334 (44.1)
Product demand	50 (13.4)	30 (10.2)	6 (6.7)	86 (11.3)
Competitors' prices	116 (31.0)	106 (36.1)	30 (33.3)	252 (33.2)
Market conditions	40 (10.7)	26 (8.8)	14 (15.6)	80 (10.6)
Consumers' paying capacity	0 (0.0)	4 (1.4)	2 (2.2)	6 (0.8)
Total responses	374 (100.0)	294 (100.0)	90 (100.0)	758 (100.0)

(Figures in parentheses are percentages of total responses.)

is most relevant in the case of units belonging to the small size-group and the least in the case of those belonging to the large size-group. The consideration of competitors' prices is the second most important factor affecting price setting, which holds good in the case of all the size-groups. It is most relevant in the case of medium size-group and the least in the case of small size-group. While the consideration of consumers' paying capacity is of no consequence for the units belonging to all the three size-groups, product demand and market conditions are almost equally important factors at the overall level. Ignoring minor variations, the latter two factors are equally important in the case of small and medium size-groups as well. Market conditions are, however, more important than product demand in the case of large size-group. Interestingly, production cost and product demand both tend to become less important in their influence on price-setting as the assets size of the firms increases.

The position above holds good largely for different product-groups as well. This is borne out by Table 4.4, which gives the distribution of total responses of sample units of different

TABLE 4.4

Distribution of Total Responses of Sample Units of Different Product-groups According to Factors Influencing Price-Setting

Factors	Product-groups				
	Chemicals	Textiles	Engineering	Metals	Food-Wood
1	2	3	4	5	6
Cost of production	60 (39.0)	52 (47.3)	100 (49.0)	76 (40.0)	46 (46.0)
Product demand	10 (6.5)	10 (9.1)	20 (9.8)	28 (14.7)	16 (16.0)
Competitors' prices	64 (41.5)	34 (30.9)	64 (31.4)	66 (34.7)	26 (26.0)

1	2	3	4	5	6
Market conditions	18 (11.7)	14 (12.7)	18 (8.8)	18 (9.5)	12 (12.0)
Consumers' paying capacity	2 (1.3)	0 (0.0)	2 (1.0)	2 (1.0)	0 (0.0)
Total responses	154 (100.0)	110 (100.0)	204 (100.0)	190 (100.0)	100 (100.0)

(Figures in parentheses are percentages of total responses.)

product-groups according to the factors affecting price-setting. It is evident that the cost of production and the competitors' prices are the two most important factors which are considered while fixing prices in all the product-groups. Except in the case of chemicals, cost of production is considered relatively more important than competitors' prices in the remaining product-groups. Consumers' paying capacity again being of hardly any relevance in any product-group, the consideration of product demand is relatively less relevant than market conditions in chemicals and textiles, and the reverse obtains in the remaining three product-groups.

4.3 PRICING POLICIES

Pricing policies provide the needed framework in which a firm can make reasonable, practicable, and effective pricing decisions. It has been observed that firms with well defined set of pricing policies usually do find it convenient to make better pricing decisions than those having no clear-cut pricing policies.

A firm may choose to charge a single price or multiple prices for the same product item. Following a single price policy means that the firm does not differentiate between customers. Such a price policy leaves no scope for negotiation or bargaining. Discounts and concessions, if allowed, are granted on equal terms to all the buyers. On the other hand, a multiple price policy when followed means that different prices are charged from different customers, depending on the type of customers, size of purchases, terms of purchases, and geographical regions. Which of these two policies is better, depends on the nature of the product, the nature of business, the objective of the firm, etc.

To bring out the similarities and the dissimilarities as to which of these two policies is more predominantly used among the various size-groups and product-groups, the sample units have been classified accordingly on the basis of their response, as in Tables 4.5 and 4.6. Table 4.5, which gives the distribution of sample units belonging to the various

TABLE 4.5

Distribution of Sample Units of Various Size-groups According to the Type of Price Policy Used

Price policies	Size-groups			
	Small	Medium	Large	Total
1	2	3	4	5
Single price policy	105 (52.5)	98 (71.1)	34 (80.9)	232 (61.0)
Multiple price policy	95 (47.5)	40 (28.9)	8 (19.1)	148 (39.0)
Total	200 (100.0)	138 (100.0)	42 (100.0)	380 (100.0)

(Figures in parentheses are percentages of the respective column totals.)

size-groups according to the type of price policy used, shows that at the overall level there is a much greater use of single price policy than multiple price policy. This also holds for the units belonging to all the three size-groups. It is significant to note that the increase in asset size of the firms is associated with a rise in the proportion of units using single price policy and, consequently, a decline in the proportion of those using multiple price policy.

The position according to the various product-groups, as revealed by Table 4.6, is essentially the same insofar as the single price policy is in much greater use than multiple price policy in all the product-groups, except engineering. Single price policy is most popular in chemicals, followed, in a descending order, by food-wood, textiles, metals, and engineering. The margin of difference between the proportion of units using single price policy and that of those using multiple price policy is the highest in the case of chemicals and the lowest in metals. In textiles and food-wood, the proportion of units using multiple price policy is about half of those using single price policy.

TABLE 4.6

Distribution of Simple Units of Different Product-groups According to the Type of Price Policy Used

Price policies	Product-groups				
	Chemicals	Textiles	Engineering	Metals	Food-Wood
1	2	3	4	5	6
Single price policy	60 (85.7)	36 (66.7)	44 (40.7)	52 (57.8)	40 (69.0)
Multiple price policy	10 (14.3)	18 (33.3)	64 (59.3)	38 (42.2)	18 (31.0)
Total	70 (100.0)	54 (100.0)	108 (100.0)	90 (100.0)	58 (100.0)

(Figures in parentheses are percentages of the respective column totals.)

4.4 PRICE CHARGED IN RELATION TO COMPETITORS' PRICES

The prices charged by the competitors serve as an important basis for fixation of the selling price of a product. No producer/manufacturer can afford to ignore the most competitive price prevailing in the market while deciding the selling price of his own product(s). A firm may have the following three alternatives to choose from: (i) to charge a price which is below the price charged by the major competitor, (ii) to charge a price equal to that of the major competitor, and (iii) to charge a price which is above the price charged by the major competitor. The position of small-scale units in regard to their choices among the three alternatives is summarized in Tables 4.7 and 4.8.

Table 4.7 gives the distribution of sample units of various size-groups according to the three choices. It shows that

TABLE 4.7

Distribution of Sample Units of Various Size-groups According to the Price Charged in Relation to Major Competitors' Price

Alternative choices	Size-groups			
	Small	Medium	Large	Total
1	2	3	4	5
Below the major competitor's price	28 (14.0)	12 (8.7)	10 (23.8)	50 (13.2)
Above the major competitor's price	24 (12.0)	18 (13.0)	10 (23.8)	52 (13.7)
Equal to the major competitor's price	148 (74.0)	108 (78.3)	22 (52.4)	278 (73.1)
Total	200 (100.0)	138 (100.0)	42 (100.0)	380 (100.0)

(Figures in parentheses are percentages of the total.)

on the whole the majority (73.1%) of the sample units charge the same price as charged by their major competitors. This is true of units belonging to all the three size-groups. The proportion of units which follow the same price as charged by the major competitor is the highest in the medium size-group, followed closely by the small size-group and, with a wide margin, the large size-group.

The other two choices are much less used in all the size-groups. The proportion of units which charge prices lower than those of their major competitor is more than that of those charging prices higher than those of their major competitor. While the reverse obtains in the case of medium size-group, the two choices turn out to be equally preferable in the large size-group. A significant point that appears to have emerged is that the tendency to fix prices above those charged by the major competitor gets stronger as the assets size tends to increase. This is quite understandable insofar as it is reflective of the fact that a firm can decide prices of its products independently of the prevailing prices as it grows in terms of asset size.

Table 4.8, which brings out the results according to various product-groups, shows that the policy of charging price equal

TABLE 4.8

Distribution of Sample Units of Different product-groups According to the Price Charged in Relation to Major Competitors' Price

Alternative choices	Product-groups				
	Chemicals	Textiles	Engin-eering	Metals	Food-Wood
1	2	3	4	5	6
Below the major competitor's price	12 (17.1)	8 (14.8)	16 (14.8)	8 (8.9)	6 (10.3)
Above the major competitor's price	14 (20.0)	8 (14.8)	12 (11.1)	14 (15.5)	4 (6.9)
Equal to major competitor's price	44 (62.9)	38 (70.4)	80 (74.1)	68 (75.6)	48 (82.8)
Total	70 (100.0)	54 (100.0)	108 (100.0)	90 (100.0)	58 (100.0)

(Figures in parentheses are percentages of the total.)

to that charged by the major competitor is most popular in all the product-groups as well. The relativity among different product-groups is such that this policy is followed by the maximum proportion of units belonging to food-wood, followed, in a descending order, by those in metals, engineering, textiles, and chemicals. Metals and chemicals are the two product-groups where the proportion of units charging prices above those of their major competitor is more than that of those charging prices below their major competitor. These two proportions being the same in textiles, the reverse obtains in engineering and food-wood. The proportion of units charging prices above those of their major competitor is the highest in chemicals, followed, in a descending order, by metals, textiles, engineering, and food-wood. As regards the policy of charging prices below those of the major competitor, the chemical product-group is at the top, followed, in descending order of importance, by textiles and engineering, food-wood, and metals.

4.5 FACTORS LEADING TO PRICE CHANGES

A variety of factors may compel the sellers to bring about changes in prices that may be prevailing in the market at a given point of time. Changes in the prices charged by the competitors, changes in the overall trend in market prices, decisions to introduce new items in the market, attempts at selling in the new market areas, and sales growth are some of the important factors which, individually and collectively, may necessitate price changes. Tables 4.9 and 4.10 bring out the relative importance of each of these factors according to the various size-groups and product-groups, respectively.

Table 4.9 shows that changes in prices charged by competitors is the most important factor leading to change in the prevailing prices. This is consistent with the fact brought out earlier that while fixing the prices of their products most of the sample units follow the prices charged by the major competitor. It is the changes in the overall trend in market

TABLE 4.9

Distribution of Total Responses of Sample Units of Various Size-groups According to Factors Leading to Price Changes

Factors	Size-Groups			Total
	Small	Medium	large	responses
1	2	3	4	5
Changes in competitor's prices	152 (49.4)	104 (48.4)	22 (34.4)	278 (47.5)
Changes in the overall trend in market prices	132 (42.9)	92 (43.0)	18 (28.1)	242 (41.3)
Decisions to introduce new items in the market	2 (0.6)	4 (1.9)	4 (6.3)	10 (1.7)
Selling in the new market area(s)	2 (0.6)	6 (2.8)	8 (12.5)	16 (2.7)
Attempts to boost sales	20 (6.5)	8 (3.7)	12 (18.7)	40 (6.8)
Total	308 (100.0)	214 (100.0)	64 (100.0)	586 (100.0)

(Figures in parentheses are percentages of total responses in the respective columns.)

prices which comes next, the impact of the remaining three factors in bringing about price changes being almost negligible in all the size-groups. However, these three factors are relatively more important in the case of units belonging to the large size-group than those belonging to small and medium size-groups.

The position according to different product-groups, as revealed by Table 4.10, remains essentially the same in the sense that changes in the prices charged by competitors and changes in the overall trend in market prices are the two most important factors leading to changes in the prevailing prices. Interestingly, both these factors are equally important in textiles, engineering, and food-wood product-groups because the proportion of units having changed their prices

TABLE 4.10

Distribution of Total Responses of Sample Units of Different Product-groups According to Factors Leading to Price Changes

Objectives	Product-groups				
	Chemicals	Textiles	Engin-eering	Metals	Food-Wood
1	2	3	4	5	6
Changes in competitor's prices	64 (52.5)	32 (44.5)	76 (45.8)	66 (49.2)	40 (42.6)
Changes in the overall trend in market prices	36 (29.4)	32 (44.5)	76 (45.8)	58 (43.3)	40 (42.6)
Decisions to introduce new items in the market	2 (1.7)	0 (0.0)	4 (2.4)	4 (3.0)	0 (0.0)
Selling in new market area(s)	10 (8.2)	4 (5.5)	2 (1.2)	0 (0.0)	0 (0.0)
Attempts to boost sales	10 (8.2)	4 (5.5)	8 (4.8)	6 (4.5)	12 (12.8)
Total responses	122 (100.0)	72 (100.0)	166 (100.0)	134 (100.0)	92 (100.0)

(Figures in parentheses are percentages to total responses in the respective columns.)

due to either of these two factors is the same in their case. But in the case of chemicals and metals it is the changes in competitor's prices which is relatively more important in bringing about changes in the prevailing prices. Among the remaining three factors, decisions to introduce new item(s) in the market has been the least relevant in all the product groups. Same is the case about selling in the new market area(s). The consideration of boosting sales has, however, been a relatively more important consideration leading to changes in the prevailing prices, but much less important in comparison to the changes in the competitor's prices and the overall trend in market prices.

4.6 DISCOUNTS OFFERED

Manufacturers and sellers usually offer a variety of discounts with manifold objectives such as increase in the volume of sales, prompt recovery of payments due from debtors, disposal of old stock, etc. The most common forms of discounts offered include cash discounts, quantity discounts, seasonal discounts, and special discounts.

The position with regard to the offer of these discounts according to various size-groups is shown in Table 4.11. On the whole, there are 48.4 per cent of the sample units which do not offer any kind of discount. This proportion is

TABLE 4.11

Distribution of Total Responses of Sample Units of Various Size-groups According to Type of Discounts Offered

Discounts offered	Size-groups			
	Small	Medium	Large	Total
1	2	3	4	5
Quantity discounts	52 (41.3)	44 (40.0)	10 (27.8)	106 (38.9)
Cash discounts	56 (44.4)	54 (49.1)	24 (66.7)	134 (49.3)
Seasonal discounts	18 (14.3)	8 (7.3)	2 (5.5)	28 (10.3)
Special discounts	0 (0.0)	4 (3.6)	0 (0.0)	4 (1.5)
Total responses	126 (100.0)	110 (100.0)	36 (100.0)	272 (100.0)
Proportion of units offering no discounts	52%	47.8%	33.3%	48.4%

(Figures in parentheses are percentages of total responses in the respective columns.)

the highest (52%) in the small size-group, 47.8 per cent in

the medium size-group, and the lowest (33.3%) in the large size-group. It is, thus, evident that the practice of offering various types of discounts tends to become more popular with the increasing in the asset size of the units. Among such units, cash discounts are the most popular, followed, in a descending order of importance, by quantity discounts and, with a wide margin, seasonal discounts. The use of special discounts is very limited. All this holds good for units belonging to all the size-groups, with the addition that special discounts are not used at all in the case of small and large size-groups.

Table 4.12, which gives the distribution of sample units of different product-groups according to the type of discounts

TABLE 4.12

Distribution of Total Responses of Sample Units of Different product-groups According to the Type of Discounts Offered

Discounts offered	Product-groups				
	Chemicals	Textiles	Engin-eering	Metals	Food-Wood
1	2	3	4	5	6
Quantity discounts	38 (46.3)	12 (27.3)	24 (48.0)	24 (34.3)	8 (30.8)
Cash discounts	42 (51.2)	30 (68.2)	20 (40.0)	30 (42.9)	12 (46.1)
Seasonal discounts	2 (2.5)	2 (4.5)	6 (12.0)	14 (20.0)	4 (15.4)
Special discounts	0 (0.0)	0 (0.0)	0 (0.0)	2 (2.8)	2 (7.7)
Total responses	82 (100.0)	44 (100.0)	50 (100.0)	70 (100.0)	26 (100.0)
Proportion of units offering no discounts	25.7%	37.0%	63.0%	44.4%	65.5%

(Figures in parentheses are percentages of total responses in the respective columns.)

offered, shows that the proportion of units offering no discounts is the highest (65.5%) in food-wood, followed by engineering, metals, textiles, and chemicals where it is the lowest. Further, the use of cash discounts is most common in the case of all the product-groups, except engineering where quantity discounts are more popular than cash discounts. Quantity discounts hold the second position and seasonal discounts, with a substantial margin, the third position. Comparing the various product-groups, quantity discounts are used by the maximum proportion of units belonging to engineering, followed, in a descending order, by those belonging to chemicals, metals, food-wood and textiles. Offer of cash discounts is most popular in the case of textiles, followed in a descending order, by chemicals, food-wood, metals, and engineering.

Chapter V

Advertising, Personal Selling and Sales Promotion

Modern marketing is not confined merely to developing a quality product, tagging it with an attractive price, and making it readily available to the customers. In order that the product is acceptable in the market, the producer must dissipate all information regarding its existence, special features, and other use characteristics among the target customers. In that sense, every producer must eventually play the role of a promoter and communicator.

As a communicator, the producer has to communicate effectively with all those who are directly or indirectly involved in the flow of the product from the producer to the final customers. This includes dealers and suppliers, external public including stock-holders, and the various government agencies. The basic objective which a producer seeks to achieve by establishing communication with all these parties is to generate goodwill for the product and its makers, and to create such reputation and trustworthiness in the minds of the actual and potential customers as would establish an edge over the rival products.

The role of the producer as a promoter and communicator has assumed so much of importance that the question whether or not to promote a given product item is no longer relevant. In fact, more crucial these days is the question as to how much to spend on promotion and in what ways to spend. The communicational role can be best performed by using various communicational tools which include advertising, personal selling, and various other sales activities which come under *sales promotion*. Known as the three primary elements or components of promotion mix, here we shall bring out the promotional practices followed by the small-scale industries in respect of these elements of promotion.

5.1 RELATIVE IMPORTANCE OF THE THREE COMPONENTS

To begin with, we shall bring out the relative importance of each of the three elements in the promotion mix according to the various size-groups and product-groups. Table 5.1 gives the distribution of sample units of various size-groups

TABLE 5.1

Distribution of Sample Units of Various Size-groups According to Three Elements of Promotion Mix

Elements of promotion mix	Size-groups: Small	Medium	Large	Total
1	2	3	4	5
Advertising	102	76	30	208
	(51.0)	(55.1)	(71.4)	(54.7)
Sales promotion	38	100	42	180
	(19.0)	(72.5)	(100.0)	(47.4)
Personal selling	52	38	14	104
	(26.0	(27.5)	(33.3)	(27.4)
Total	200	138	42	380

(Figures in parentheses are percentages of the total number of units in the respective columns.)

according to whether or not they are engaged in advertising, sales promotion, and personal selling. It reveals that personal selling is the least popular element of promotional mix for the units belonging to the medium and large size-groups, and sales promotion for those belonging to the small size-group. Advertising, on the other hand, is most popular in the case of small size-group, while sales promotion is so in the case of medium and large size-groups. As the asset size increases, all the three elements of promotion mix tend to be more frequently used. On the whole, however, advertising is the most frequently used means of promotion, followed, with a narrow margin, by sales promotion, and personal selling which is the least popular.

The position according to different product-groups is not much different. It may be observed from Table 5.2 that

TABLE 5.2

Distribution of Sample Units of Different Product-groups According to Three Elements of Promotion Mix

Elements of promotion mix	Product-group: Chemicals	Textiles	Engineering	Metals	Food-Wood
1	2	3	4	5	6
Advertising	62 (88.6)	28 (51.8)	60 (55.6)	32 (35.6)	26 (44.8)
Sales promotion	60 (85.7)	36 (66.7)	36 (33.3)	28 (31.1)	20 (34.5)
Personal selling	42 (60.0)	14 (29.9)	18 (16.7)	24 (26.7)	6 (10.3)
Total	80	54	108	90	58

(Figures in parentheses are percentages of the total number of units in the respective columns.)

advertising is the most popular means of promotion in all the product-groups, except for textiles where sales promotion has an edge over advertising. There is no such exception in the case of personal selling which is the least popular promotional tool in all the product-groups. As between different product-groups, advertising is most frequently used in chemicals, followed, with a wide margin, by engineering, textiles, food-wood and, metals where it is least used. The chemical product-group is ahead of all others in personal selling as well, followed by textiles and, with a very wide margin, by engineering, food-wood, and metals.

5.2 PROMOTIONAL EXPENSES IN RELATION TO SALES

We may now examine the relativity between the three components of promotion mix in terms of the expenses incurred on each, both according to the various size-groups and product-groups. Table 5.3 gives the distribution of total

TABLE 5.3

Distribution of Promotional Expenses and Sales per Unit (Rs.'000) According to Various Size-groups

Particulars	Size-groups			
	Small	Medium	Large	Total
1	2	3	4	5
Advertising expenses	5.02 (39.8)	11.17 (43.7)	23.33 (47.5)	9.28 (43.4)
Sales promotion expenses	1.20 (9.5)	1.57 (6.1)	8.43 (17.2)	2.13 (10.0)
Personal selling expenses	6.41 (50.7)	12.89 (50.2)	17.33 (35.3)	9.97 (46.6)
Total promotional expenses	12.6	25.6	49.1	21.4
Annual sales	1498	3985	5253	2813
Proportion of promotional expenses to total sales	0.84%	0.64%	0.93%	0.76%

(Figures in parentheses are percentages.)

promotional expenses according to the various size-groups. It shows at the overall level that the highest (46.6%)

proportion of total promotional expenses goes to personal selling, 43.4 per cent to advertising, and the lowest, just 10 per cent, to sales promotion. A similar pattern obtains in the case of units belonging to the small and medium size-groups. The large size-group presents a different picture insofar as the proportion of total promotional expenses is the highest on advertising (47.5%), followed by the proportion of expenses on personal selling (35.3%), and that of on sales promotion.

As between the various size-groups, the proportion of advertising expenses has continuously increased with the increase the asset size from 39.7 per cent in the small size-group to 47.5 per cent in the large size-group. Contrary to this, the proportion of personal selling expenses has declined from 50.7 per cent in the small size-group to 35.5 per cent in the large size-group. Expenses on sales promotion constitutes the lowest proportion in the medium size-group and the highest in the large size-group. It is interesting that on an average each unit spends just 0.76 per cent of sales on promotion. As compared to this, promotional expenses as proportion of sales per unit are the lowest (0.64%) in the medium size-group, 0.84 per cent in the small size-group, and the highest (0.93%) in the large size-group.

The position according to different product-groups, as revealed by Table 5.4, is essentially the same insofar as the proportion of promotional expenses per unit is the highest on personal selling and the lowest on sales promotion in all the product-groups, except for engineering and food-wood where it is the reverse that obtains. The margin of difference between the highest and the lowest is the maximum in the case of textiles, followed by metals and chemicals.

Across different product-groups, the proportion of promotional expenses on advertising is the highest in engineering, followed, with a wide margin, by food-wood, chemicals, metals, and textiles. The proportion of personal selling expenses is the highest in textiles, followed by metals, chemicals, food-wood, and engineering. Sales promotion expenses constitute the highest proportion in food-wood, followed by textiles, chemicals, metals and engineering. Total promotional expenses as percentage to sales per unit are the maximum (1.78%) in the case of chemicals, followed, in a descending order, by engineering (0.70%), textiles (0.45%), metals (0.36%), and the least in food-wood (0.13%).

Finally, a cross-classification of the sample units according to sales and promotional expenses as presented in Table 5.5, permits us to compute the coefficient of correlation

TABLE 5.4

Distribution of Promotional Expenses and Sales per Unit (Rs.'000) According to Different Product-groups

Particulars	Product-groups				
	Chemicals	Textiles	Engineering	Metals	Food-Wood
1	2	3	4	5	6
Advertising expenses	23.75 (37.4)	1.96 (20.0)	13.23 (63.1)	2.48 (36.4)	1.86 (39.7)
Sales promotion expenses	7.20 (11.3)	1.85 (18.9)	0.96 (4.6)	0.49 (7.2)	1.00 (21.3)
Personal selling expenses	32.57 (51.3)	6.00 (61.1)	6.80 (32.3)	3.89 (56.4)	1.83 (39.0)
Total promotional expenses	63.5 (100.0)	9.8 (100.0)	21.0 (100.0)	6.8 (100.0)	4.7 (100.0)
Annual sales	3567	2780	2980	1886	3616
Proportion of promotional expenses to total sales	1.78%	0.45%	0.70%	0.36%	0.13%

(Figures in parentheses are percentages.)

(r) by using the formula $r = \dfrac{\Sigma fd_x d_y - \dfrac{(\Sigma fd_x)(\Sigma fd_y)}{N}}{\left[\Sigma fd_x^2 - \dfrac{(\Sigma fd_x)^2}{N}\right]\left[\Sigma fd_y^2 - \dfrac{(\Sigma fd_y)^2}{N}\right]}$

When calculated, r = 0.303. Square root of r gives us the coefficient of determination $R^2 = r^2 = (0.303)^2 = 0.09181$. This means that at the overall level promotional expenses explain variations in sales only to the extent of 9 per cent. However, the application of t test yields a t value (t_c = 6.18) which is more than the tabulated t value at 1 per cent level

TABLE 5.5

Cross-classification of Sample Units According to Sales and Promotional Expenses

	Promotional expenditure (Y) (Rs. '000)							
Sales(X) (Rs. lac)	0-10	10-30	30-60	60-100	100-150	150-210	210-280	Total Units
1	2	3	4	5	6	7	8	9
0-10	114	10	12	0	0	0	0	136 (35.8)
10-30	84	16	14	6	0	0	0	124 (32.6)
30-60	34	22	10	10	4	2	0	82 (21.6)
60-100	8	6	0	4	0	0	2	20 (5.3)
100-150	2	2	2	0	2	2	2	12 (3.1)
150-210	4	2	0	0	0	0	0	6 (1.6)
Total units	246	58	38	20	6	4	8	380 (100.0)
	(64.7)	(15.3)	(10.0)	(5.3)	(1.6)	(1.1)	(2.1)	(100)

(Figures in parentheses are percentages.)

of significance. This means that there is a significant positive association between promotional expenses and sales.

5.3 ADVERTISING

Advertising consists of non-personal form of communication. It is one of the most effective multi-purpose tools of direct persuasion of the target customers. The basic purpose of advertising is to enhance the responsiveness of potential buyers to an organization and its offerings.

5.3.1 *Methods of Deciding Advertising Budget*

How much is to be spent on advertising (i.e., advertising budget) is one of the crucial decisions to be taken under advertising. The three commonly used methods of deciding advertising budget are: (i) Affordable method, (ii) Percentage of sales method, and (iii) Competitive parity method. The position with regard to the methods used by the small-scale units is as shown in Tables 5.6 and 5.7.

Table 5.6, which gives the distribution of sample units of various size-groups according to the methods used for deciding

TABLE 5.6

Distribution of Sample Units of Various Size-groups According to Methods Used for Deciding Advertising Budget

Method	Size-groups			
	Small	Medium	Large	Total
1	2	3	4	5
Affordable method	60 (58.8)	20 (26.3)	0 (0.0)	80 (38.5)
Percentage of sales method	20 (19.6)	14 (18.4)	24 (80.0)	58 (27.9)
Competitive parity method	22 (21.6)	42 (55.3)	6 (20.0)	70 (33.7)
Total	102 (100.0)	76 (100.0)	30 (100.0)	208 (100.0)

(Figures in parentheses are percentages of their respective totals.)

the advertising budget, shows that the majority of the units in the small size-group use *affordable* method, followed by those using the *competitive parity* method, and the *percentage of sales* method. In the medium size-group the competitive parity method is most widely used, followed by the affordable method, and percentage of sales method. In the large size-group, 80 per cent of the firms use percentage of sales method, and the remaining 20 per cent use competitive parity method. The affordable method is not used at all by the units belonging to this size-group. On the whole, however, the affordable method is used most frequently, followed by the competitive parity method, and percentage of sales method.

Distribution of sample units according to different product-groups and the methods used for preparing advertising budget, as in Table 5.7, shows that the affordable method is

TABLE 5.7

Distribution of Sample Units of Different Product-groups According to Methods Used for Deciding Advertising Budget

Methods	Product-groups				
	Chemicals	Textiles	Engineering	Metals	Food-Wood
1	2	3	4	5	6
Affordable method	12 (19.4)	10 (35.7)	38 (63.3)	0 (0.0)	20 (76.9)
Percentage of sales method	34 (54.8)	0 (0.0)	14 (23.3)	10 (31.3)	0 (0.0)
Competitive parity method	16 (25.8)	18 (64.3)	8 (13.4)	22 (68.7)	6 (23.1)
Total	62 (100.0)	28 (100.0)	60 (100.0)	32 (100.0)	26 (100.0)

(Figures in parentheses are percentages of totals.)

least used in chemicals, and most in engineering and food-wood. It is not at all used in metals. The percentage of sales method is most popular in chemicals, and the competitive parity method in textiles and metals. While the percentage of sales method is not at all used in textile and food-wood product-groups, the affordable method has the same position in the case of metals.

5.3.2 *Advertising Objectives*

Of the several objectives which advertising may be directed to achieve, providing support to personal selling and other forms of promotion is the most common. As in the case of large-scale industries, the common objectives which small-scale industries seek to achieve through advertising are such as increasing sales/profit, creating brand awareness, neutralizing competition, and introducing new item(s) in the market.

The responses received on the relative importance of each of these objectives have been given ranks on the basis of scores assigned to them. The final outcome according to various size-groups is as shown in Table 5.8. It may be observed at the overall level that increasing sales/profit and

TABLE 5.8

Ranking of Advertising Objectives According to Various Size-groups

Advertising objectives	Size-groups							
	Small		Medium		Large		Overall	
	Scores	Rank	Scores	Rank	Scores	Rank	Scores	Rank
1	2	3	4	5	6	7	8	9
Increasing sales/profit	274	1	210	1	72	3	556	1
Creating brand awareness	90	2	102	2	76	1	268	2

1	2	3	4	5	6	7	8	9
Neutralizing competitor's advertising	30	4	46	4	30	3	106	4
Introducing new items	16	5	28	5	28	4	72	5
Selling in new market area(s)	60	3	48	3	20	5	128	3

(Here ranks have been determined on the basis of score values. The response choices being 'generally', 'occasionally', and 'never', score values have been obtained by assigning weights equal to 2,1, and 0, respectively.)

creating brand awareness are the two most important advertising objectives as they get the first and second rank, respectively. This is true of the units belonging to the small and medium size-groups as well. In the case of large size-group, the order of importance of these two objectives is reverse. The objective of selling in new market area(s), neutralizing competitor's advertising, and introducing new item(s) in the market get the third, fourth, and fifth position, respectively, at the overall level as well as in both the small and medium size-groups. The order of importance of these objectives obtaining in the case of large size-group is different in that neutralizing competitor's advertising, introducing new item(s) in the market, and selling in the new market area get the third, fourth, and fifth rank, respectively.

Table 5.9 brings out the relative importance of different advertising objectives in different product-groups. It may be noted that increasing sales/profit is the most popular objective in all the product-groups. This is followed very closely in all the product-groups by the objective of creating brand awareness. While these are the two most sought-after objectives in the case of chemicals, followed by engineering, the remaining product-groups are almost at par in this respect. Among the remaining three advertising objectives, neutralizing competitor's advertising and selling in the new market area are relatively more important in the case of chemicals and engineering than they are in the remaining product-groups. Advertising as a means of introducing new item(s) in the market holds the lowest position in all the product-groups, but it is relatively more popular in chemicals than in the other product-groups.

TABLE 5.9

Ranking of Advertising Objectives According to Different Product-groups

Advertising objectives	Product-groups									
	Chemicals		Textiles		Engineering		Metals		Food-Wood	
	Scores	Rank	Scores	Rank	Scores	Rank	Scores	Rank	Scores	Rank
1	2	3	4	5	6	7	8	9	10	11
Increasing sales/profit	176	1	74	1	156	1	78	1	72	1
Creating brand awareness	120	2	34	2	60	2	26	2	28	2
Neutralizing competitors' advertising	50	3	12	5	24	4	10	3	10	4
Introducing new item(s) in the market	34	5	14	4	10	5	6	5	8	5
Selling in the new market area(s)	48	4	22	3	34	3	8	4	16	3

(Here ranks have been determined on the basis of score values. Score values have been obtained by assigning weights as in Table 5.8.)

5.3.3 *Advertising Media Used*

Depending upon their form, benefits, and coverage, a firm can engage itself in advertising by using varied media, such as magazines and newspapers, radio and television, outdoor displays, direct mail, catalogues, directories, circulars, etc. Each of these media differs in terms of the extent of its reach, frequency, and impact on the target buyers. Before an advertising media is selected, it is necessary that the media planner collects all possible information about each media and their use characteristics in relation to the type of product, type of customers, media cost, etc.

Given the various factors affecting media selection, it will be useful to know that the media use pattern in small-scale units according to various size-groups and product-groups. Table 5.10 classifies the responses received from the sample units of various size-groups according to broad categories of media used. It shows at the overall level that 54.7 per cent

TABLE 5.10

Distribution of Responses of Sample Units of Various Size-groups According to Advertising Media Used

Advertising media	Size-groups			
	Small	Medium	Large	Total
1	2	3	4	5
Total units	200	138	42	380
Number of units engaged	102	76	30	208
in advertising	(51.0)	(57.1)	(71.4)	(54.7)
Radio/TV	0	2	2	4
	(0.0)	(2.6)	(6.7)	(1.9)
Newspapers/magazines	54	62	30	146
	(52.9)	(81.6)	(100.0)	(70.2)
Wall writings/posters	40	22	8	70
	(39.2)	(28.9)	(26.7)	(33.7)
Outdoor hoardings	28	24	12	64
	(27.5)	(31.6)	(40.0)	(30.8)
Direct mail/	22	32	12	66
letter writing	(21.5)	(42.1)	(40.0)	(31.7)
Directories, cinema	48	38	20	106
slides, etc.	(47.1)	(50.0)	(66.7)	(51.0)

(Figures in parentheses are percentages of the number of units engaged in advertising.)

(208 units) of the total sample units are engaged in advertising. Out of them, 70 per cent advertise through newspapers and magazines, and about 51 per cent through other sources such as directories, cinema slides, etc. Wall writings/posters, outdoor hoardings, and direct mail/letter writing are used by 34 per cent, 31 per cent, and 32 per cent of those engaged in advertising, respectively. Radio and TV are the least popular media as these are used only by about 2 per cent of the units engaged in advertising.

Out of 200 sample units belonging to the small size-group, 51 per cent (102) have been found to be engaged in advertising. With 138 and 42 units belonging to the medium and large size-groups, respectively, the proportion of those engaged in advertising is 57 per cent (76 units) in the case of the former, and 71 per cent (30 units) in the case of the latter. The overall media use pattern among those engaged in advertising is the same in all the three size-groups as at the overall level insofar as newspapers and magazines are the most commonly used media. It is followed by other media consisting of directories and cinema slides, etc. Radio and TV being the least used media, the remaining three media as compared to newpapers and magazines have been used in a limited way without much variations as between the three size-groups.

Except in the case of wall writings and posters where the proportion of user firms has declined with the increase in asset size, the proportion of users of other categories of media has shown a tendency to increase as we move from units of small asset size to those of medium and large asset size. Obviously, it follows that the small-scale units prefer to make much greater use of low cost media because of their inability to earmark more funds for advertising. With whatever small amount they are able to spare for the purpose, the small units try to reach their target markets by adopting cheaper media sources such as newspapers, magazines, directories, cinema slides, etc. The use of radio and TV is too costly to be within their reach. However, as the asset-size tends to increase, the financial position of the small units improves and the use of TV and radio increases.

Table 5.11, which gives the media use position according to different product-groups, shows that of the total number

TABLE 5.11

Distribution of Responses of Sample Units of Different Product-groups According to Advertising Media Used

Advertising media	Product-groups				
	Chemicals	Textiles	Engin-eering	Metals	Food-Wood
1	2	3	4	5	6
Total units	70	54	108	90	58
Number of units engaged in advertising	62 (88.6)	28 (51.9)	60 (55.6)	32 (35.6)	26 (44.8)
Radio and TV	4 (6.5)	0 (0.0)	0 (0.0)	0 (0.0)	0 (0.0)
Newspapers/magazines	40 (64.5)	20 (71.4)	54 (90.0)	18 (56.3)	14 (53.8)
Wall writings/ posters	22 (35.5)	6 (21.4)	18 (30.0)	14 (43.8)	10 (38.5)
Outdoor hoardings	28 (45.2)	10 (35.7)	12 (20.0)	10 (31.3)	4 (15.4)
Direct mail/ letter writing	18 (29.0)	10 (35.7)	20 (33.3)	12 (37.5)	6 (23.1)
Directories, cinema slides, etc.	26 (41.9)	16 (57.1)	36 (60.0)	18 (56.3)	10 (38.5)

(Figures in parentheses are percentages to the total number of units engaged in advertising.)

of sample units belonging to the various product-groups, the proportion of those engaged in advertising is the highest (88.6%) in chemicals, followed, in a descending order, by 55.6 per cent in engineering, 51.9 per cent in textiles, 44.8 per cent in food-wood, and 35.6 per cent in metals. Overall media use pattern obtained in different product-groups is the same as for the various size-groups in the sense that newspapers and magazines are the most commonly used media, followed by other cheaper media sources such as directories, cinema slides, etc., in all the product-groups. The least used media consist of direct mail/letter writing in chemicals, wall writings and posters in textiles, and outdoor hoardings in engineering, metals, and food-wood. The use of radio and TV is wholly absent in all the product-groups, except in chemicals where the proportion of user units is just 5.7 per cent.

Among various product-groups, the use of newspapers and magazines as advertizing media is the highest in engineering, followed by textiles, chemicals, metals, and food-wood. Use of directories, cinema slides, etc. among the various product-groups follows the same order. The proportion of units using wall writings and posters is the highest in metals, followed, in a descending order, by food-wood, chemicals, engineering, and textiles. In the case of outdoor hoardings, the chemical product-group is at the top, followed by textiles, metals, engineering, and food-wood where its use in minimum. Direct mail/letter writing is most frequently used in metals, followed, in a descending order, by textiles, engineering, chemicals, and food-wood.

5.3.4. *Preparation of Advertising Message*

The effectiveness of advertising as a tool of communication depends largely on the message which is intended to be conveyed. It is, therefore, necessary that adequate care is observed in developing the advertising message so that it meets the requirements of being desirable, acceptable and effective. So important is the role of advertising message in achieving promotional objectives that large firms spend a huge amount of money in engaging the services of specialized agencies to get their advertising message prepared.

The practice of engaging the services of professional artists or specialized agencies is, however, not very common especially in the case of smaller units. The reason being that these units are neither adequately aware of the role that advertising message plays in sales promotion, nor do they have the necessary wherewithals to make use of specialized services. Therefore, the only alternative available to them is to do the job themselves. To bring out the relative use of the two choices in preparing the advertising message, the sample responses have been presented according to size-groups in Table 5.12, and according to product-groups in Table 5.13.

Table 5.12 shows that about 90.2 per cent of the units belonging to the small size-group prepare their advertising message themselves or have it done by their staff, and the remaining 9.8 per cent use the services of advertising agencies or professional artists. In the medium and large size-groups, the proportion of units which prepare their advertising message themselves or get it done through their staff is 73.7 per cent and 40 per cent, respectively. Accordingly, the services of specialized advertising agencies are used by 28.3 per cent of the units belonging to the medium size group and

TABLE 5.12

Preparation of Advertising Message in Various Size-groups

Message preparer	Size-groups			
	Small	Medium	Large	Total
1	2	3	4	5
Self or own staff	92 (90.2)	56 (73.7)	12 (40.0)	160 (76.9)
Advertising agencies or professional artists	10 (9.8)	20 (28.3)	18 (60.0)	48 (23.1)
Total	102 (100.0)	76 (100.0)	30 (100.0)	208 (100.0)

(Figures in parentheses are percentages.)

60 per cent of those belonging to the large size-group. On

the whole, advertising message is self-prepared or by the staff in the case of three-fourth of the firms, the remaining one fourth utilize specialized services for the purpose. Interestingly, again, the expected pattern follows here also. That is, the use of the services of specialized agencies/ professional artists increases with the increase in asset size.

Table 5.13 brings out that the proportion of units which prepare their advertising message themselves or through their staff is the highest in the case of metals, followed by textiles, food-wood, engineering, and chemicals. The order based on the proportion of units using the services of specialized agencies is reverse, the highest being in chemicals and the lowest in metals.

TABLE 5.13

Preparation of Advertising Message in Different Product-groups

Message prepared	Product-groups				
	Chemicals	Textiles	Engineering	Metals	Food-Wood
1	2	3	4	5	6
Self or own staff	40 (64.5)	24 (85.7)	44 (73.3)	30 (93.7)	22 (84.6)
Advertising agencies or professional artists	22 (35.5)	4 (14.3)	16 (26.7)	2 (6.3)	4 (15.4)
Total	62 (100.0)	28 (100.0)	60 (100.0)	32 (100.0)	26 (100.0)

(Figures in parentheses are percentages.)

5.3.5 *Advertising Coverage*

Advertising coverage refers to the geographical area which a manufacturer intends to reach through advertising. It is often defined in terms of geographical boundaries of the market identified as local, regional, national, or international which a producer may serve. When advertising coverage is so viewed, we do expect some interesting results so far as the small-scale units are concerned.

Table 5.14 gives the classification of sample units belonging to various size-groups according to their advertising coverage either being local, regional, national, or international. It shows that out of 208 sample units which have been found engaged in advertising, 41.4 per cent have national coverage, 34.6 per cent local coverage, 16.3 per cent regional coverage and only 7.7 per cent international coverage. In the case of units belonging to the small size-group, the highest proportion of them have local coverage, followed, with a very wide margin, by those having national, regional, and international coverage. Among those belonging to the medium size-group,

TABLE 5.14

Distribution of Sample Units of Various Size-groups According to Advertising Coverage

Coverage	Size-groups			
	Small	Medium	Large	Total
1	2	3	4	5
Local	56 (54.9)	14 (18.4)	2 (6.7)	72 (34.6)
Regional	18 (17.7)	12 (15.8)	4 (13.3)	34 (16.3)
National	24 (23.5)	44 (57.9)	18 (60.0)	86 (41.4)
International	4 (3.9)	6 (7.9)	6 (20.0)	16 (7.7)
Total	102 (100.0)	76 (100.0)	30 (100.0)	208 (100.0)

(Figures in parentheses are percentages to their respective column totals.)

the proportion of units having national coverage is the highest and those having international coverage is the lowest. Local coverage is limited to 18.4 per cent of the units and regional coverage to 15.8 per cent. In the large size-group, the highest proportion of units have national coverage, followed by those having international, regional and local coverage. These results are important inasmuch as they reflect that regional and, more so, local coverage tend to decline and national and international coverage tend to increase with the increase in the asset size of the firms.

Table 5.15, which gives the position on advertising coverage according to different product-groups, shows that the proportion of units having national coverage is the highest and those having regional coverage the lowest in chemicals and engineering. In the case of metals and food-wood, the

TABLE 5.15

Distribution of Samples Units of Different Product-groups According to Advertising Coverage

Coverage	Product-groups				
	Chemicals	Textiles	Engineering	Metals	Food-Wood
1	2	3	4	5	6
Local	16 (25.8)	4 (14.3)	18 (30.0)	20 (62.6)	14 (53.8)
Regional	10 (16.1)	8 (28.6)	6 (10.0)	6 (18.7)	4 (15.4)
National	36 (58.1)	8 (28.6)	6 (46.7)	6 (18.7)	4 (30.8)
International	0 (0.0)	8 (28.5)	8 (13.3)	0 (0.0)	0 (0.0)
Total	62 (100.0)	28 (100.0)	60 (100.0)	32 (100.0)	26 (100.0)

(Figures in parentheses are percentages of their respective column totals.)

highest proportion of units have local coverage. Regional and national coverage is the same in metals and textiles, the former being the lowest in food-wood. While there is no international coverage in chemical, metal and food-wood product-groups, 28.6 per cent of the units have international coverage in textiles and 13.3 per cent in engineering.

5.4 PERSONAL SELLING

Personal selling is a critically important element of promotional mix which consists of making use of the services of salesmen in a variety of ways. Salesmen are often referred to as unsung heroes of the success of a firm in its marketing efforts, for it is the initiative and skill with which the salesmen work which determine, to a large extent, the successful implementation of any marketing programme. Inspite of the crucial role personal selling plays in increasing sales, the small-scale units are not in a position to engage the services of salesmen and use personal selling in their promotional mix. Table 5.16 which gives the classification of sample units belonging to various .size-groups into users and

TABLE 5.16

Distribution of Sample Units of Various Size-groups According to Users and Non-users of Sales Force

Particulars	Size-groups			
	Small	Medium	Large	Total
1	2	3	4	5
Sales force users	52 (26.0)	38 (27.5)	14 (33.3)	104 (27.4)
Sales force non-users	148 (74.0)	100 (72.5)	28 (67.7)	276 (72.6)
Total	200 (100.0)	138 (100.0)	42 (100.0)	380 (100.0)

(Figures in parentheses are percentages of the respective column totals.)

non-users of personal selling, shows that at the overall level the proportion of sample units using personal selling is much less than that of its non-users. This is true of all the size-groups, though the margin of difference between the proportion of users and non-users narrows down as the asset size increases. This is because the proportion of users increases as we move from small to large size-groups. That is, the users of personal selling constitute the smallest and the non-users the highest proportion in the small size-group, and the order reverses as we move on to the large size-group.

The position according to various product-groups, as revealed by Table 5.17, is essentially the same for all the product-groups except in the case of chemicals. While the proportion of users of personal selling is more than that of

TABLE 5.17

Distribution of Sample Units of Different Product-groups According to Users and Non-users of Sales Force

Particulars	Product-groups				
	Chemicals	Textiles	Engineering	Metals	Food-Wood
1	2	3	4	5	6
Sales force users	42 (60.0)	14 (25.9)	18 (16.7)	24 (26.7)	6 (10.3)
Sales force non-users	28 (40.0)	40 (74.1)	90 (83.3)	66 (73.3)	52 (89.7)
Total	70 (100.0)	54 (100.0)	108 (100.0)	90 (100.0)	58 (100.0)

(Figures in parentheses are percentages of the respective column totals.)

non-users in chemicals, it is the reverse that obtains in the case of the remaining product-groups. The margin of difference between the proportion of users and non-users is maximum in food-wood, followed by engineering, textiles, and metals. That is, the users constitute the highest proportion in chemicals, followed, with a wide margin, by metals, textiles, engineering, and food-wood. The order reverses in the case of non-users.

5.4.1 *Salesforce Functions*

It has been observed that the small scale units use personal selling with varied objectives. While some of them use the services of salesmen with the sole purpose of selling, others engage them for seeking sales orders, providing delivery, collecting payments, introducing new item(s) to dealers and/or customers, collecting market information, etc.

In order to bring out the relative importance of these functions according to various size-groups, we may refer to Table 5.18 which gives the classification of total responses

TABLE 5.18

Distribution of Total Responses of Sample Units of Various Size-groups According to the Functions Performed by Salesmen

Functions	Size-groups			
	Small	Medium	Large	Total
1	2	3	4	5
Seeking orders	52 (100.0)	38 (100.0)	14 (100.0)	104 (100.0)
Providing delivery	40 (76.9)	30 (78.9)	14 (100.0)	84 (80.8)
Collecting payments	52 (100.0)	38 (100.0)	14 (100.0)	104 (100.0)
Introducing new items to dealers/customers	32 (61.5)	28 (73.7)	8 (57.1)	68 (65.4)
Gathering market information	48 (92.3)	32 (84.2)	10 (71.4)	90 (86.5)
Total units which employ sales Force	52	38	14	104

(Figures in parentheses are percentage of the total units which employ sales force.)

of sample units using personal selling in their promotional mix according to different functions. It is interesting to note that all sample units falling in the three size-groups utilize the services of sales force mainly for seeking orders and collecting payments. In the small size-group, 92 per cent of the units use sales force to gather market information, while in the medium and large size-groups it is 84.7 per cent and 71.4 per cent, respectively. Providing delivery gets the third place in all the size-groups, followed by the use of sales force to introduce new items to the dealers and/or the customers.

The position according to different product-groups, as revealed by Table 5.19, is essentially the same. As before, seeking sales orders and collecting payments are the two

TABLE 5.19

Distribution of Total Responses of Sample Units of Different Product-groups According to the Functions Performed by Salesmen

Functions	Product-groups				
	Chemicals	Textiles	Engineering	Metals	Food-Wood
1	2	3	4	5	6
Seeking orders	42 (100.0)	14 (100.0)	18 (100.0)	24 (100.0)	6 (100.0)
Providing delivery	36 (85.7)	14 (100.0	14 (77.8)	16 (66.7)	4 (66.7)
Collecting payments	42 (100.0)	14 (100.0)	18 (100.0)	24 (100.0)	6 (100.0)
Introducing new items to dealers/ customers	24 (57.1)	12 (85.7)	16 (88.9)	12 (50.0)	4 (66.7)
Gathering market information	36 (85.7)	12 (85.7)	18 (100.0)	18 (75.0)	6 (100.0)
Total units which employ sales force	42	14	18	24	6

(Figures in parentheses are percentages of the total units which employ sales force.)

main objectives which the salesforce is geared to achieve, followed, in a descending order, by gathering market information, providing delivery, and introducing new items to the dealers.

5.5 SALES PROMOTION

Sales is not a self-generating activity. Cut-throat competition among rival firms for winning away the major share of a given market has enhanced the importance of sales promotion as an element of promotion mix. It consists of all those activities which stimulate sales and increase the effectiveness of advertising and personal selling. Sales promotion consists of those selling activities which are of non-recurring nature such as trade shows and exhibitions, demonstrations, free gifts, distribution of free samples, etc. with a view to generating immediate sales.

Table 5.20, which gives the classification of sample units according to different sales promotion activities for units

TABLE 5.20

Distribution of Sample Units of Various Size-groups According to Sales Promotion Activities

Sales promotion activities	Size-groups			
	Small	Medium	Large	Total
1	2	3	4	5
Total sample units	200	138	42	380
Number of sample units engaged in sales promotion activities	42 (21.0)	96 (69.6)	42 (100.0)	180 (47.4)
Number of sample units not engaged in sales promotion activities	158 (79.0)	42 (30.4)	0 (0.0)	200 (52.6)
Free gifts/samples	32 (76.2)	80 (83.3)	28 (66.7)	140 (77.8)

1	2	3	4	5
Participation in trade fairs/exhibitions	2 (4.8)	0 (0.0)	8 (19.0)	10 (5.5)
Cooperative advertising	4 (9.5)	12 (12.5)	2 (4.8)	18 (10.0)
Special discounts	4 (9.5)	4 (4.2)	4 (9.5)	12 (6.7)

(Figures in parentheses are percentages.)

belonging to the various size-groups, shows that out of 380 sample units only 47.4 per cent (180 units) are engaged in sales promotion activities. This proportion is the lowest (21%) in the small size-group, 69.6 per cent in the medium size-group, and the highest (100%) in the large size-group. A majority of them (77.8%) at the overall level resorts to supplying free gifts/ samples. The proportion each of those participating in trade fairs/exhibitions, cooperative advertising, and allowing special discounts varies between 5 to 10 percent. This holds good for units belonging to all the size-groups, barring those participating in trade fairs/exhibitions in the case of large size-group. Interestingly, the proportion of units offering free gifts/samples is the highest (83.3%) in the medium size-group, 76.2 per cent in the small size-group and the lowest (66.7%) in the large size-group.

According to Table 5.21, which gives the position of different product-groups, the proportion of sample units engaged in different sales promotion activities is the highest in chemicals (85.7%) followed by textiles, food-wood, engineering, and metals where it is the lowest (31.1%). As before, providing free-gifts/samples is the most popular sales promotion activity in all the product-groups, with textiles at the top, followed, in a descending order, by metals, chemicals, engineering, and food-wood. Among the remaining sales promotion activities, cooperative advertising comes next in chemicals and food-wood, special discounts in textiles and metals, and participation in trade fairs/exhibitions in engineering. Again, participation in trade fairs/exhibitions is completely absent in textiles and metals, cooperative advertising in engineering, and special discounts in food-wood.

TABLE 5.21

Distribution of Sample Units of Different Product-groups According to Sales Promotion Activities

Sales promotion activities	Product-groups				
	Chemicals	Textiles	Engin-eering	Metals	Food-Wood
1	2	3	4	5	6
Total sample units	70	54	108	90	58
Number of sample units engaged in sales promotion activities	60 (85.7)	36 (66.6)	36 (33.7)	28 (31.1)	20 (34.5)
Number of sample units not engaged in sales promotion activities	10 (14.3)	18 (33.7)	72 (66.3)	62 (68.9)	38 (5.5)
Free gifts/samples	44 (73.3)	32 (88.9)	26 (72.2)	24 (85.7)	14 (70.0)
Participation in trade fairs/exhibitions	2 (3.3)	0 (0.0)	6 (16.7)	0 (0.0)	2 (10.0)
Cooperative advertising	10 (16.7)	2 (5.5)	0 (0.0)	2 (7.1)	4 (20.0)
Special discounts	4 (6.7)	2 (5.6)	4 (11.1)	2 (7.2)	0 (0.0)

(Figures in parentheses are percentages.)

Chapter VI

Channel Decisions

Distribution is concerned with the performance of those activities which are necessary for transferring goods from the producers to the final buyers or the users. Apart from transportation and storage of goods, it also consists of promotional and financial activities that are performed to assist the transfer of ownership of the product from the producer to the customers.

Owing to enlargement in the size of market, producers generally do not sell their products directly to the final buyers. Instead, the services of a host of marketing intermediaries are used in the course of flow of products to the final users. These intermediaries are of two types: (i) Merchant middlemen, and (ii) Agent middlemen. Merchant middlemen include wholesalers and retailers who buy, take title to, and resell the merchandise. Agent middlemen, on the other hand, are those engaged in assisting and negotiating sales or purchase or both on behalf of their principals (buyers, sellers, or both). They include brokers, commission houses, manufacturers, agents, auctioneers, etc. Apart from these, there are different service agencies such as transportation companies, independent warehouses, banks, and advertising agencies, which also assist in the distribution of goods from the producer to the final buyers. However, they neither take title to goods, nor negotiate sales or purchases.

Channel decisions are critical decisions as they exercise powerful influence on the remaining elements of the marketing mix. This is because of two reasons. First, the channel selected for a company's products affects every other marketing decision. For example, pricing decisions depend on whether a firm seeks a few franchised high mark-up dealers or mass distribution. Similarly, advertising decisions of a firm are greatly influenced by the degree of cooperation received from channel members, the middlemen. Second, channel decisions involve a firm in relatively long-term commitments. For example, a television manufacturer, who may have signed with independent franchise dealers in the selling of his televisions, cannot easily replace them with company-owned outlets even if changed conditions have necessitated it.

In this chapter we shall bring out a few important aspects relating to channel decisions, such as the number of channel levels used, distribution intensity, factors affecting channel selection, etc.

6.1 CHANNEL LEVELS

Every institution which performs some function(s) by way of assisting product flow from the producer to customers constitutes a channel level. The length of a channel is defined in terms of the number of intermediary levels between the producer and customers. The various commonly used channels are:

i) Zero-level channel (Manufacturer to Consumers),
ii) One-level channel (Manufacturer to Retailers/Agents to Consumers),
iii) Two-level channel (Manufacturer to Wholesalers to Retailers to Consumers), and
iv) Three-level channel (Manufacturer to Wholesalers to Jobbers to Retailers to Consumers).

To know the relative use of these channels by the small-scale units, we may refer to Table 6.1 which gives the distribution of sample units of various size-groups according

TABLE 6.1

Distribution of Sample Units of Various Size-groups According to Channel Levels Used

Channels levels	Size-groups			
	Small	Medium	Large	Total
1	2	3	4	5
Zero-Level Channel: Manufacturer to Consumers/Users	76 (38.0)	54 (39.1)	18 (42.9)	148 (38.9)
One-Level Channel: Manufacturer to Retailers/ Agents to Consumers	70 (35.0)	40 (29.0)	16 (38.1)	126 (33.2)
Two-Level Channel: Manufacturer to Wholesalers to Retailers to Consumers	54 (27.0)	44 (31.9)	8 (19.0)	106 (27.9)
Total	200 (100.0)	138 (100.0)	42 (100.0)	380 (100.0)

(Figures in parentheses are percentages of totals.)

to the number of channel levels used. It shows that on the whole 38.9 per cent of the sample units sell directly to the final consumers/users, 33.2 per cent use one level channel of distribution, and the remaining (27.9%) have adopted two level channel. There are no sample units using three level or more than three-level channel to distribute their products to the final users. Among those belonging to the small size-group, zero-level channel is used by 38 per cent of the units, one-level channel by 35 per cent, and the two-level channel by the remaining 27 per cent. The channel use pattern in the large size-group is largely the same as in the small size-group. That is, the highest proportion (42.9%) of units use zero-level channel and the lowest (19.0%) use two-level channel, the use of one-level channel extending to the remaining 38.1 per cent of the units. The medium size-group presents a different picture in the sense that while zero-level channel is still used by the highest proportion (39.1%) of units, it is the one-level channel whose users now constitute the lowest proportion (29%).

As between the various size-groups, the proportion of units selling through zero-level channel is the highest (42.9%) in the case of large size-group and the lowest (38%) in the small size-group. This appears to indicate that the use of zero-level channel tends to increase with the increase in the asset-size of firms. No definite pattern follows in the case of the other two channels. While the proportion of units using one-level channel is the highest in the large size-group, it is the lowest in the case of medium size-group. The reverse obtains about the use of two-level channel.

The channel usage pattern according to different product-groups is shown in Table 6.2 The chemical product-group has the highest proportion (48.6%) of units using two-level channel, followed by that of those using zero-level channel. Almost a similar pattern obtains in the case of textiles in the sense that the proportion of units using two-level channel is the highest, the same (44.4%) as that of those using one-level channel, and that of those using zero-level channel is the least (11.2%). Engineering and metal product-groups follow different channel use pattern as the proportion of units using zero-level channel is the highest and that of those using two-level channel is the lowest in both these product-groups. The use of one-level channel is the maximum and that of two-level channel the least in food-wood.

Among the various product-groups, zero-level channel is used most frequently in engineering, followed by metals, food-wood, chemicals, and textiles. Food-wood is at the top in the use of one level channel, followed by textiles, metals, chemicals, and engineering. The two-level channel being most popular in chemicals, it is followed, in a descending order, by textiles, metals, engineering, and food-wood.

TABLE 6.2

Distribution of Sample Units of Different Product-groups According to Channel Levels Used

Channel levels	Product-groups					
	Chemicals	Textiles	Engin-eering	Metals	Food-Wood	Total
1	2	3	4	5	6	7
Zero-Level Channel: Manufacturer to consumers/Users	18 (25.7)	6 (11.2)	64 (59.2)	42 (46.7)	18 (31.0)	148 (39.0)
One-Level Channel: Manufacturer to Retailers/Agents to Consumers	18 (25.7)	24 (44.5)	24 (22.3)	30 (33.3)	30 (51.7)	126 (33.1)
Two-Level Channel: Manufacturer to Wholesalers to Retailers to Consumers	34 (48.6)	24 (44.4)	20 (18.5)	18 (20.0)	10 (17.3)	106 (27.9)
Total	70 (100.0)	54 (100.0)	108 (100.0)	90 (100.0)	58 (100.0)	380 (100.0)

(Figures in parentheses are percentages to the totals.)

6.2 DISTRIBUTION INTENSITY

Having decided the number of channel levels, the seller has to decide upon the appropriate number of middlemen whose services should be used at each channel level. Any decision taken in this regard is influenced by the degree of market exposure sought to be achieved by a firm. The number of middlemen whose services are to be used along the distribution path defines the 'distribution intensity'. It is in terms of the degree of distribution intensity that distribution is classified either as mass distribution, selective distribution, or exclusive distribution.

Mass distribution provides maximum sales exposure to a

product. A manufacturer must use multiple channels to achieve mass distribution intensity. Generally, the manufacturers of convenience goods such as cigarettes, sugar, etc., adopt this system. Exclusive distribution involves use of the services of a single middleman, for example, a retailer in each market area. Producers of speciality goods such as readymade garments, shoes, televisions, etc., usually adopt this system. Mass distribution and exclusive distribution being the two extremes, manufacturers prefer to follow the selective distribution system which combines the advantages of the two. The chief characteristic of selective distribution policy is that it restricts the number of outlets to be provided at each distribution level. Manufacturers of shoes, clothing, automobiles, etc. adopt this system. Generally, it is the selective distribution system which is considered to be the best alternative.

The data presented in Tables 6.3 and 6.4 offer interesting results about the degree of distribution intensity used by the small-scale industries. Table 6.3, which gives the needed information according to various size-groups, shows at the overall level that apart from 39 per cent (148) of our sample units where no well-defined distribution channels are used, mass distribution system is the most popular and exclusive distribution the least used system among channel users. Selective distribution is also fairly popular as it is used by 20.5 per cent of the sample units as compared to 37.9 per cent of those using the mass distribution system. This particularly holds good in the case of units belonging to the small size-group. Medium and large size-groups present a different picture to the extent that in their case it is the selective distribution policy which has been adopted by the highest proportion of units. The exclusive distribution policy is least popular as in the case of small size-group.

Among the three size-groups, the proportion of units using mass distribution is the highest in the small size-group and the lowest in the large size-group. The selective distribution system is used by the highest proportion of units belonging to the medium size-group, followed very closely, by that of those comprising the large and, with a wide margin, the small size-group. The proportion of units using exclusive distribution is the highest (4.8%) in the large size-group and the lowest (1.0%) in the small size-group. In brief, the use of exclusive distribution tends to increase and that of mass distribution tends to decline with the increase in asset size.

TABLE 6.3

Distribution of sample Units of Various Size-groups According to Degree of Distribution Intensity

Distribution intensity	Size-groups			
	Small	Medium	Large	Total
1	2	3	4	5
Mass distribution	98	36	10	144
	(49.0)	(26.1)	(23.8)	(37.9)
Selective distribution	24	42	12	78
	(12.0)	(30.4)	(28.6)	(20.5)
Exclusive distribution	2	6	2	10
	(1.0)	(4.4)	(4.8)	(2.6)
Distribution Channel	76	54	18	148
non-users	(38.0)	(39.1)	(42.8)	(39.0)
Total	200	138	42	380
	(100.0)	(100.0)	(100.0)	(100.0)

(Figures in parentheses are percentages of total.)

The position according to different product-groups is evident from Table 6.4. It shows that mass distribution system is most popular in all the product-groups, with the addition that the proportion of units using this system is the same as that of those using the selective distribution in engineering. Further, the mass distribution system is used by the highest proportion of units belonging to textiles, followed, in a descending order, by food-wood, chemicals, and metals and engineering where it is the lowest. The selective distribution which gets the second position in terms of its use frequency in all the size-groups, is the most popular in textiles, followed, very closely, by chemicals, food-wood, engineering and metals. While exclusive distribution is not used at all in metals and food-wood, it has been adopted by 3.7 per cent of the units belonging to textiles and engineering each, and 5.7 per cent of the units in chemicals.

TABLE 6.4

Distribution of Sample Units of Different Product-groups According to Degree of Distribution Intensity

Distribution intensity	Product-groups				
	Chemicals	Textiles	Engineering	Metals	Food-Wood
1	2	3	4	5	6
Mass distribution	28 (40.0)	30 (53.6)	20 (18.5)	36 (40.0)	28 (48.3)
Selective distribution	20 (28.6)	16 (29.6)	20 (18.5)	12 (13.3)	12 (20.7)
Exclusive distribution	4 (5.7)	2 (3.7)	4 (3.7)	0 (0.0)	0 (0.0)
Distribution channel non-users	18 (25.7)	6 (11.1)	64 (59.3)	42 (46.7)	18 (31.0)
Total	70 (100.0)	54 (100.0)	108 (100.0)	90 (100.0)	58 (100.0)

(Figure in parentheses are percentages to totals.)

6.3 FACTORS AFFECTING THE SELECTION OF MIDDLEMEN

The selection of middlemen through whom a product eventually reaches the ultimate users is made keeping in view a number of factors. Goodwill of the middlemen in the market, their financial position, level of promotional support they are prepared to give to the product, cost of using various intermediaries, availability of warehousing facilities, etc. are some of the important factors affecting the choice of middlemen. The relative importance of each of these factors is revealed by the data presented in Tables 6.5 and 6.6.

Table 6.5, which gives the distribution of sample units of various size-groups according to the factors affecting the selection of middlemen, shows at the overall level that goodwill of the middlemen for the manufacturer is the most important factor as it is kept in view by the highest proportion of sample units while selecting the middlemen. Financial position of the middlemen which comes next is followed, in a descending order of importance, by the consideration of willingness to provide promotional support to the product, cost of using various types of

TABLE 6.5

Distribution of Sample Units of Various Size-groups According to Factors Affecting the Selection of Middlemen

Factors considered	Size-groups			
	Small	Medium	Large	Total
1	2	3	4	5
Goodwill	114 (30.2)	72 (34.9)	30 (32.6)	216 (31.9)
Financial position	102 (27.0)	44 (21.4)	18 (19.6)	164 (24.3)
Promotional support to the product	80 (21.2)	42 (20.4)	24 (26.1)	146 (21.6)
Cost	62 (16.4)	38 (18.4)	16 (17.4)	116 (17.2)
Warehousing facilities	20 (5.2)	10 (4.9)	4 (4.3)	34 (5.3)
Total	378 (100.0)	206 (100.0)	92 (100.0)	676 (100.0)

(Figures in parentheses are percentages of totals.)

middlemen, and the availability of warehousing facilities with the middlemen. The order of importance of these factors is the same in all the size-groups, except that the consideration of financial position of the middlemen gets the third position and that of willingness to provide promotional support to the product the second position in the large size-group. While the considerations of financial position and availability of warehousing facilities are most important in the case of units belonging to the small size-group, willingness to give promotional support is so in the case of units belonging to the large size-group. Interestingly, to those belonging to the large-size group financial position and warehousing facilities are the least important considerations.

The order of importance of the various factors remains the same even when viewed according to different product-groups. Table 6.6 clearly reveals that goodwill of the middlemen, which is kept in view while selecting them by the highest proportion of units in all the product-groups,

TABLE 6.6

Distribution of Sample Units of Different Product-groups According to Factors Affecting the Selection of Middlemen

Factors considered	Product-groups				
	Chemicals	Textiles	Engineering	Metals	Food-Wood
1	2	3	4	5	6
Goodwill	50 (32.5)	42 (35.6)	46 (27.4)	42 (36.8)	36 (29.5)
Financial position	46 (29.9)	26 (22.1)	42 (25.0)	28 (24.6)	22 (18.0)
Promotional support to the product	34 (22.1)	24 (20.3)	36 (21.4)	18 (14.8)	34 (27.9)
Cost	24 (15.5)	24 (20.3)	34 (20.2)	14 (12.3)	20 (16.4)
Warehousing facilities	0 (0.0)	2 (1.7)	10 (6.0)	12 (10.5)	10 (8.2)
Total	154 (100.0)	118 (100.0)	168 (100.0)	114 (100.0)	122 (100.0)

(Figures in parentheses are percentages of totals.)

followed, in a descending order of importance, by considerations of financial position of the middlemen, willingness to provide promotional support to the product, cost of using various types of middlemen, and the availability of warehousing facilities. The variations among different product-groups are not too sharp to invite specific mention in respect of any of these factors.

6.4 MOTIVATING MIDDLEMEN

How well a product sells in the market depends to a large extent on the interest and involvement of middlemen in pushing through the product. It is, therefore, necessary that the middlemen whose services are used in the distribution process are people adequately and genuinely motivated. Since the system leaves enough scope both for cooperation and conflict between the producers and distributors (the middlemen), the task of motivating the middlemen is rather difficult and complex. The job of motivating them to put in their best must start with an attempt on the part of the manufacturer to understand the needs and psychology of the type of middlemen selected to work at different channel levels. The common forms of incentives and facilities used by the manufacturers for the purpose include higher margin, favourable contract deals, premium, cooperative advertising allowance, display allowance, sales contests, etc. To have an idea of the practices prevailing in the small-scale industries regarding the use of these incentives, the responses sought from the respondent units have been presented in Table 6.7 according to the various size-groups, and in Table 6.8 according to different product-groups.

Table 6.7 clearly shows that easy credit terms is the most important incentive which is allowed to the middlemen to draw them into the distribution system. True in the case of all the three size-groups, it is followed, in a descending order of importance, by the incentive of replacement of defective items, cooperative advertising, free gifts, and special discount.

The variations among the three size-groups are in no case wide enough to require mention. However, it is significant to note that the incentives of cooperative advertising and replacement of defective items tend to lose importance, and the facilities of easy credit terms, free gifts, and special discount tend to gain importance, with the increase in asset size.

TABLE 6.7

Distribution of Total Scores of Sample Units of Various Size-groups According to Incentives Used for Seeking Middlemen's Support

Incentives	Size-groups			
	Small (Scores)	Medium (Scores)	Large (Scores)	Total responses
1	2	3	4	5
Cooperative advertising	56	62	32	150
	(15.3)	(15.0)	(14.4)	(15.9)
Free gifts	28	34	18	80
	(7.6)	(8.2)	(8.1)	(8.0)
Special discounts	16	20	12	48
	(4.4)	(4.8)	(5.4)	(4.8)
Easy credit terms	196	222	120	538
	(53.6)	(53.6)	(54.1)	(53.7)
Replacement of defective items	70	76	40	186
	(19.3)	(18.4)	(18.0)	(18.6)
Total scores	366	414	222	1002
	(100.0)	(100.0)	(100.0)	(100.0)

(Figures in parentheses are percentages of total scores in the respective columns.)

The relative positions of various incentives and facilities in attracting and motivating the right kind of middlemen does not change much when viewed according to different product-groups. As shown in Table 6.8, the incentive of easy credit terms is used by the highest proportion of sample units in all the product-groups. Agreement to replace defective items is the second most important incentive in all the groups, except in chemicals where the second place goes to cooperative advertising. The facility of cooperative advertising gets the third place in engineering and second in food-wood, fourth in textiles, and the lowest in metals. The place of free gifts is fourth in chemicals and engineering, third in textiles and metals, and fifth, the lowest, in food-wood. While the incentive of special discounts is the least important in chemicals, textile, and engineering product-groups, it gets the fourth position in metals and food-wood.

TABLE 6.8

Distribution of Total Scores of Sample Units of Different Product-groups According to Incentives Used for Seeking Middlemen's Support

Incentives	Product-groups				
	Chemicals	Textiles	Engineering	Metals	Food-Wood
1	2	3	4	5	6
Cooperative advertising	42 (26.9)	8 (8.3)	15 (12.9)	1 (1.3)	9 (15.0)
Free gifts	10 (6.4)	9 (9.4)	10 (8.6)	7 (9.6)	4 (6.7)
Special discounts	6 (3.9)	3 (3.1)	6 (5.2)	4 (5.5)	5 (8.3)
Easy credit terms	68 (43.6)	64 (66.7)	59 (50.9)	43 (58.9)	35 (58.3)
Replacement of defective items	30 (19.2)	12 (12.5)	26 (22.4)	18 (24.7)	7 (11.7)
Total scores	156 (100.0)	96 (100.0)	116 (100.0)	73 (100.0)	60 (100.0)

(Figures in parentheses are percentage of total scores in the respective columns.)

Across different product-groups, the incentive of easy credit terms is most popular in textiles, followed, in a descending order, by metals, food-wood, engineering, and chemicals. The facility to replace defective items is most popular in metals, followed by engineering, chemicals, textiles, and food-wood. While cooperative advertising is most popular in chemicals and least in metals, the variations among various product-groups are not significant in the case of facilities of free gifts and special discounts.

Chapter VII

Some Other Issues

In this chapter we shall bring out the marketing practices in respect of those aspects which have not been covered under any of the preceeding four chapters (III to VI). These relate to sales forecasting, market segmentation, credit facilities, and inventories.

7.1 SALES FORECASTING

Sales forecasting plays an important role in the process of planning and implementation of marketing policies and programmes. By its very nature, business is characterized by uncertainties which give rise to the risk of losses. Although the risk factor cannot be eliminated altogether, it can be reduced substantially through effective planning and scientific budgeting. Sales forecasting provides the necessary basis for the preparation of an action plan in that direction.

Sales forecast can be seen as a statement showing the quantities or values of sales projected into the future product-wise, area-wise, and/or period-wise. It serves as the most useful information for decision making for all firms irrespective of whether they are big or small. Salesmen are assigned sales quotas keeping sales forecasts for different territories in view. Production budget, cash budget, and capital budget are all prepared on the basis of sales forecasts. Almost all marketing decisions whether relating to product, pricing, channel selection, or promotion are backed by sales forecasting.

There are several methods of sales forecasting. Important among them are : (i) Discussion with the customers, (ii) Estimates made by the sales force, (iii) Past behaviour of sales, (iv) Overall market trend, etc. It will be useful to have a knowledge of the methods that are being followed by the sample units for sales forecasting.

Table 7.1, which gives the distribution of responses of

TABLE 7.1

Distribution of Responses of Sample Units of Various Size-groups According to Methods Used for Sales Forecasting

Forecasting methods	Size-groups			Total
	Small	Medium	Large	responses
1	2	3	4	5
Discussion with buyers	34	38	10	82
	(10.2)	(17.9)	(13.5)	(13.3)
Salesforce estimates	12	26	8	46
	(3.6)	(12.3)	(10.8)	(7.4)
Overall market trend	50	26	16	92
	(15.1)	(12.3)	(21.6)	(14.9)
Past sales behaviour	150	66	22	238
	(45.2)	(31.1)	(29.7)	(38.5)
Government Policies	86	56	18	160
	(25.9)	(26.4)	(24.4)	(25.9)
Total responses	322	212	74	618
	(100.0)	(100.0)	(100.0)	(100.0)
A. Total units which forecast sales	150	112	34	296
	(75.0)	(81.2)	(81.0)	(77.9)
B. Total units which do not forecast sales	50	26	8	84
	(25.0)	(18.8)	(19.0)	(22.1)

(Figures in parentheses are percentages of total responses, and those in A and B rows are percentages to the total number of units in the sample.)

sample units of various size-groups according to the methods used for sales forecasting, shows the following:

i) On the whole, about 78 per cent of the units have adopted sales forecasting as a regular marketing activity. This proportion is the lowest (75%) in the small size-group, and the highest (81.2%) in the medium size-group.

ii) Past behaviour of sales serves as the most important basis of sales forecasting both at the overall level as also for units belonging to the three size-groups. Similarly, estimates of sales based on information about government policy constitute the second most popular method of sales forecasting in all the size-groups and at the overall level. In the small and large size-groups, overall market trend, discussion with customers, and sales force estimates get the third, fourth and fifth positions, respectively, in order of importance. In the medium size-group, discussion with customers gets the third place. The overall market trend and salesforce estimates lag far behind with a tie. Sales forecasting based on the estimates of sales force is least popular in all the three size-groups. It is mainly because a large number of the small units do not often engage the services of salesman.

iii) Past behaviour of sales is the most commonly used basis of making sales forecast at the overall level and in each size-group. Information about government policies as the basis of sales forecasting comes next, again at both the levels. Estimation of sales on the basis of market trend is most popular in the large size-group and least so in the medium size-group.

The position according to different product–groups, is that the proportion of units engaged in sales forecasting is the maximum in the case of chemicals, followed by food-wood, textiles, engineering, and metals where it is the minimum. The picture is essentially the same insofar as the past behaviour of sales is the most widely used method of sales forecasting in all the product-groups. It is most popular in metals, followed, in a descending order, by food-wood, engineering, chemicals and textiles. Information about government policies serves as the second most important

TABLE 7.2

Distribution of Responses of Sample Units of Different Product-groups According to Methods Used for Sales Forecasting

Forecasting method	Product-groups				
	Chemicals	Textiles	Engineering	Metals	Food-Wood
1	2	3	4	5	6
Discussion with buyers	32 (21.6)	8 (9.8)	22 (11.8)	14 (10.6)	6 (8.6)
Salesforce estimates	22 (14.9)	2 (2.4)	14 (7.5)	8 (6.1)	0 (0.0)
Overall market trend	24 (16.2)	14 (17.1)	22 (11.8)	18 (13.7)	14 (20.0)
Past sales behaviour	44 (29.7)	24 (29.3)	74 (39.8)	64 (48.5)	32 (45.7)
Government policies	26 (17.6)	34 (41.4)	54 (29.1)	28 (21.1)	18 (25.7)
Total responses	148 (100.0)	82 (100.0)	186 (100.0)	132 (100.0)	70 (100.0)
A. Total units which forecast sales	65 (9.28)	46 (85.2)	77 (71.3)	57 (63.3)	51 (87.9)
B. The units which do not forecast sales	5 (7.2)	8 (14.8)	31 (28.7)	33 (36.7)	7 (12.1)

(Figures in parentheses are percentages of total responses, and those in A and B rows are percentages of the total number of units in the sample.)

basis of sales forecasting in all the product-groups, except chemicals where it is the discussion with the buyers which gets the second place. Among the remaining product-groups, information about government policies is most frequently used as the basis of sales forecasting in textiles, followed by engineering, food-wood, and metals where it is least used.

Overall market trend gets the third place and discussion with buyers the fourth place in order of importance in textiles, engineering, metals, and food-wood. Sales force estimates are the least used basis of sales forecasting in all the product-groups, particularly in textiles and food-wood. The use of overall market trend as the basis of sales forecasting is most frequent in food-wood, followed, very closely, by textiles, chemicals, metals, and engineering. Sales forecasting based on discussion with customers is made most frequently in chemicals, followed, with a wide margin, by engineering, metals, textiles, and food-wood.

7.2 MARKET SEGMENTATION—GEOGRAPHICAL COVERAGE

A market segment consists of a number of buyers who possess common characteristics to make a distinct group. Market segmentation, on the other hand, is the process of dividing the total market for a product into different parts. As no two buyers of a product are ever identical in all respects, it is a concept which is derived from the characteristic of markets being heterogeneous. The marketing significance of segmentation is that it enables the management to improve its ability to tailor its products and marketing programmes according to the requirement of each segment.

Markets can be segmented on various bases such as geographical area, income, age, education, life style, etc. It has been observed in the course of collection of information that most of the entrepreneurs are unaware of market segmentation as a concept and its benefits. They were, however, able to describe the geographical coverage of their markets in terms of a district, state, country as a whole, or extending to foreign countries. Though even this kind of geographical coverage is different from what segmentation on geographical basis really implies, yet it would be useful to bring out the similarities and differences according to such geographical coverage.

Table 7.3, which gives the distribution of sample units of various size-groups according to geographical coverage,

TABLE 7.3

Distribution of Sample Units of Various Size-groups According to Geographical Coverage

Market coverage	Size-groups			
	Small	Medium	Large	Total
1	2	3	4	5
Local coverage (district)	80 (40.0)	24 (17.4)	4 (9.5)	108 (28.4)
State coverage	36 (18.0)	44 (31.9)	10 (23.8)	90 (23.7)
National coverage	76 (38.0)	60 (43.5)	20 (47.6)	156 (41.1)
International coverage	8 (4.0)	10 (7.2)	8 (19.1)	26 (6.8)
Total	200 (100.0)	138 (100.0)	42 (100.0)	380 (100.0)

(Figures in parentheses are percentages of their respective column totals.)

shows that at the overall level the highest proportion (41.1%) of units have national coverage, followed by 28.4 per cent of those having local coverage, 23.7 per cent having state coverage, and the lowest (6.8%) having international coverage. Among the units belonging to the small size-group, the highest proportion (40%) of them has local coverage, followed closely by that of those having national coverage (38.0%). State coverage is limited to18 per cent of the units, while those having international coverage are just 4 per cent. In the medium and large size-groups, the proportion of units having national coverage is the highest, followed by those having state coverage. International coverage is the least in the small and medium size-group and local coverage in the large size-group.

Across the various size-groups, national coverage is enjoyed by the highest proportion of units in the large size-group and the lowest in the small size-group. The same order holds in respect of state and international coverage, the margin of difference between the highest and the lowest being too prominent in the case of the latter. Not unexpectedly, the proportion of units having local coverage is the highest (40%) in the small size-group, and the lowest (9.5%) in the large size-group. In general, local coverage declines, and the coverage at the state, national and international levels tends to rise, with the increase in the asset size of the units.

The position according to different product-groups, as revealed by Table 7.4, shows that the proportion of units having national coverage is the highest in chemicals, textiles and metals. It is followed by the proportion of units having state coverage which is the second highest in chemicals and textiles and that of those having local coverage in metals. In engineering and food-wood it is the proportion of units having local coverage which is the highest and those having national coverage the second highest. Local coverage is at the third place in chemicals and state coverage in metals. There being no international coverage in metals and food-wood, it is the lowest in chemicals, followed by engineering and metals.

TABLE 7.4

Distribution of Sample Units of Different product-groups According to Geographical Coverage

Market coverage	Product-groups				
	Chemicals	Textiles	Engineering	Metals	Food-Wood
1	2	3	4	5	6
Local coverage	5	7	37	33	26

1	2	7	4	5	6
	(7.1)	(12.9)	(34.2)	(36.7)	(44.8)
State coverage	18	11	24	22	15
	(25.7)	(20.4)	(22.2)	(24.4)	(25.9)
National coverage	44	27	33	35	17
	(62.9)	(50.0)	(30.6)	(38.9)	(29.3)
International coverage	3	9	14	0	0
	(4.3)	(16.7)	(13.0)	(0.0)	(0.0)
Total	70	54	108	90	58
	(100.0)	(100.0)	(100.0)	(100.0)	(100.0)

(Figures in parentheses are percentages of their respective column totals.)

Across different product-groups, national coverage is maximum in chemicals, followed, in a descending order, by textiles, metals, engineering, and food-wood. Contrary to this, state coverage is the highest in food-wood, followed by chemicals, metals, engineering, and textiles where it is the lowest. Local coverage is the lowest in chemicals, followed by textiles, engineering, metals, and food-wood where it is the maximum.

7.3 CREDIT FACILITIES TO BUYERS

Sellers are required to provide many a facility to the buyers to be able to stay in the market in the face of cut-throat competition. Common among these facilities are free delivery, free repair services, free installations, replacement, and credit facility, etc. Out of these, credit facility is the most important both for the buyers and the sellers. The sellers find it useful to extend credit facility because it leads to an increase in sales. The customers resort to making use of this facility as it enables them to satisfy their needs without money being paid immediately in exchange. An interesting practice which has come to notice in the course of sample survey is that extension of credit facility by the small-scale units is not voluntary. It is treated more as a compulsion since almost all dealers insist on grant of credit facility, so that any one denying this facility faces the problem of drastic fall in sales. Tables 7.5 and 7.6, which give the distribution of sample units according to different proportions of credit sales to total sales, help bring out the extent to which credit facility is extended by the small-scale units.

Table 7.5, which gives the position according to the various size-groups, shows the following:

i) At the overall level approximately one half of the units extend credit sales between 50 to 100 per cent of their total sales. This is followed by 20.5 per cent of the units which sell 25 to 50 per cent of their output on credit basis. An equal number of units do so up to 25 per cent of their sales. The proportion of units extending no credit facility is just 12 per cent.
ii) While the overall pattern in the medium and large size-groups is the same as at the overall level, the small size-group presents a slightly different picture only to the extent that the proportion of units extending credit sales between 25 to 50 per cent of their sales is the same as that of those extending no credit sales facility.

TABLE 7.5

Distribution of Sample Units of Various size-groups According to Different Proportions of Credit Sales to Total Sales

Proportion of credit sales to total sales	Size-groups			
	Small	Medium	Large	Total
1	2	3	4	5
Nil	36 (18.0)	8 (5.8)	2 (4.8)	46 (12.1)
Upto 25 per cent	46	23	5	74

1	2	3	4	5
	(23.0)	(16.7)	(11.9)	(19.5)
25 to 50 per cent	36	34	8	78
	(18.0)	(24.6)	(19.0)	(20.5)
50 per cent or more	82	73	27	182
	(41.0)	(52.9)	(64.3)	(47.9)
Total	200	138	42	380
	(100.0)	(100.0)	(100.0)	(100.0)

(Figures in parentheses are percentage of their respective column totals.)

iii) To proportion of units extending credit sales to the extent of 50 per cent or more of their sales is the maximum (64.3%) in the large size-group and the minimum (41%) in the small size-group. As against this, the proportion of those extending no credit sales facility is the maximum (18%) in the small size-group and the minimum (4.8%) in the large size-group. Same is the case with regard to the proportion of units giving credit sales upto 25 per cent of their total sales. It is the highest (23%) in the small size-group and the lowest (11.7%) in the large size-group. Those allowing credit sales between 25 per cent of their sales constitute the highest proportion in the medium size-group and the lowest in the small size-group.

The position according to different product-groups, as shown by Table 7.6, is such that the proportion of units extending credit sales to the extent of 50 per cent or more of their sales is the highest in all the product-groups, except food-wood where it is the lowest. It is followed by the proportion of units extending credit sales between 25 to 50 per cent of their sales in chemicals and textiles, and those extending credit sales upto 25 per cent of their sales in engineering and metals. Those extending credit sales upto 25% of their sales is much lower in chemicals (2.9%) and textiles (7.4%) as compared to the remaining three product-groups. The proportion of units extending no credit sales is the lowest in all the product-groups, except in food-wood where it is the maximum. Credit sales allowed upto 50 to 100 per cent of total sales is the maximum in chemicals, followed

TABLE 7.6

Distribution of Sample Units of Different product-groups According to Different Proportions of Credit Sales to Total Sales

Proportion of credit sales to total sales	Product-groups				
	Chemicals	Textiles	Engineering	Metals	Food-Wood
1	2	3	4	5	6
Nil	0 (0.0)	2 (3.7)	18 (16.7)	6 (6.7)	20 (34.5)
Upto 25 per cent	2 (2.9)	4 (7.4)	28 (25.9)	22 (24.4)	18 (31.0)
25 to 50 per cent	14 (20.0)	10 (18.5)	22 (20.4)	20 (22.2)	12 (20.7)
50 per cent or more	54 (77.1)	38 (70.4)	40 (37.0)	42 (46.7)	8 (13.8)
Total	70 (100.0)	54 (100.0)	108 (100.0)	90 (100.0)	58 (100.0)

(Figures in parentheses are percentages of their respective column totals.)

closely by textiles and, with a wide margin, metals, engineering, and food-wood. There being not much of variations among different product-groups as to the proportion of units extending credit sales between 25 to 50 per cent of sales, the proportion of those extending credit sales upto 25 per cent of sales is the maximum in food-wood, followed closely by engineering and metals, and, with a wide margin, by textiles and chemicals.

7.4 INVENTORY

Inventories are reservoirs of goods held in anticipation of

sales. Though the sales of a product follow a continuous process, yet they fluctuate considerably from time to time. The amount of ready stock is a matter of paramount importance for marketeer inasmuch as it involves taking decisions about the maximum and minimum inventory levels. These two limits are decided keeping in view (i) the anticipated sales, and (ii) the cost of holding inventory. Tables 7.7 and 7.8 give minimum and maximum inventory levels and inventory turnover ratios in respect of various size-groups and product-groups, respectively.

It is evident from Table 7.7 that the minimum inventory level is the lowest in the small size-group and the highest in the large size-group. For different size-groups maximum and average inventory levels follow a similar order. The inventory turnover ratio bears a negative relationship with asset size. It declines with the increase in the asset size of the firm.

TABLE 7.7

Size of Inventory and Inventory Turnover Ratios According to Various Size-groups

Size-groups	Minimum size (Rs.'000)	Maximum size (Rs.'000)	Average size (Rs.'000)	Inventory turnover ratio (times)
1	2	3	4	5
Small	24.02	130.97	77.49	19.3
Medium	90.14	342.34	216.24	18.4
Large	186.90	555.31	371.11	14.1

Table 7.8, which gives the position in respect of different product–groups, shows that the minimum inventory level is the highest in the units belonging to textiles, followed by engineering, chemicals, food-wood, and metals where it is the lowest. The maximum inventory level is the highest in the case of food-wood, followed, in a descending order, by textiles, engineering, chemicals, and metals. The average is

inventory held is maximum in food-wood, followed by textiles, engineering chemicals and metals. The inventory turnover

TABLE 7.8

Size of Inventory and Inventory Turnover Ratios According to Different Product-groups

Product groups	Minimum size (Rs.'000)	Maximum size (Rs. '000)	Average size (Rs. '000)	Inventory turnover ratio (times)
1	2	3	4	5
Chemicals	61.85	249.71	155.78	22.9
Textiles	75.56	275.93	175.74	12.4
Engineering	72.4	261.04	166.54	17.9
Metals	47.93	129.59	88.75	21.3
Food–Wood	59.86	392.46	226.16	16.0

ratio is the highest in the case of chemicals, followed, very closely, by metals and, with a noticeable margin, engineering, food-wood, and textiles where it is the lowest.

7.5 ELEMENTS OF MARKETING MIX—RELATIVE IMPORTANCE

The decisions affecting the marketing mix fall in four categories, each consisting of decisions relating to each of the four elements of marketing mix. Thus, a decision may either belong to the category of product decisions, promotional decisions, pricing decisions, or channel distribution. To be able to know the relative importance of each of these four categories of decisions in the overall marketing mix, responses were sought from the sample units as to which of them they consider most important, and the same are presented in Tables 7.9 and 7.10.

Table 7.9, which gives the position according to various size-groups, shows the following:

i) At the overall level 55.3 per cent of the units consider product decisions as the most important, followed by 25.3 per cent of those holding price decisions as such. While 15.2 per cent the units treat channel decisions to be the most important, promotional decisions are considered as such by the lowest (4.2%) proportion of them. The order is exactly the same in the case of units belonging to the small and medium size-groups. The large size-group presents a different picture insofar as the distribution decisions are considered most important by the lowest proportion of sample units,

TABLE 7.9

Distribution of Sample Units of Various Size-groups Holding the Various Types of Decisions as Most Important

Particulars	Size-groups			
	Small	Medium	Large	Total
1	2	3	4	5
Product decisions	126 (63.0)	64 (46.4)	20 (47.6)	210 (55.3)
Price decisions	40 (20.0)	48 (34.8)	8 (19.1)	96 (25.3)
Channel/distribution decisions	30 (15.0)	22 (15.9)	6 (14.3)	58 (15.2)
Promotional decisions	4 (2.0)	4 (2.9)	8 (19.0)	16 (4.2)
Total	200 (100.0)	138 (100.0)	42 (100.0)	380 (100.0)

(Figures in parentheses are percentages of the respective column totals.)

and the proportion of those holding promotional and pricing decisions as such being the same (19%).

ii) As between the various size-groups, product decisions are the most important for the highest proportion of units belonging to the small size-group, followed by those in the large and medium size-groups. The proportion of units which consider pricing decisions to be the most important is the highest in the medium size-group, followed by the small and large size-groups. The order being the same in the case of channel decisions, promotional decisions are considered most important by the highest proportion of units in the large size-group, followed, with a very wide margin, by the medium and small size-group.

Based on Table 7.10, the position according to different product-groups is as under:

TABLE 7.10

Distribution of Sample Units of Different Product-groups Holding the Various Type of Decisions as Most Important

Particulars	Product-groups				
	Chemicals	Tex-tiles	Engin-eering	Metals	Food-Wood
1	2	3	4	5	6
Product decisions	38 (54.3)	30 (55.6)	62 (57.4)	52 (57.8)	28 (48.3)
Pricing decisions	10 (14.3)	10 (18.5)	28 (25.9)	28 (31.1)	20 (34.5)
Channel/distribution decisions	16 (22.8)	12 (22.2)	14 (13.0)	10 (11.1)	6 (10.3)
Promotional decisions	6 (8.6)	2 (3.7)	4 (3.7)	0 (0.0)	4 (6.9)
Total	70 (100.0)	54 (100.0)	108 (100.0)	90 (100.0)	58 (100.0)

(Figures in parentheses are percentages of the respective column totals.)

i) Product decisions are viewed as most important by the highest proportion of units in all the five product-groups.

This is followed by the proportion of units which consider channel decisions as such in chemicals and textiles, and those holding price decisions as such in the case of engineering, metals and food-wood. The third place goes to pricing decisions in chemicals and textiles and to channel decisions in the remaining product-groups. Again, promotional decisions are considered most important by the lowest proportion of units belonging to all the product-groups, except metals where there is not even a single unit holding these decisions as such.

ii) Among the various product-groups, product decisions are most important for the highest proportion of units belonging to metals, followed, with a narrow margin, by those belonging to engineering, textiles, chemicals, and food-wood. Pricing decisions are considered most important by the highest proportion of units in food-wood, followed, in a descending order, by metals, engineering, textiles, and chemicals. The chemical product-group is at the top followed by textiles, engineering, metals, and food-wood, in regard to channel decisions being taken as the most important.

Chapter VIII

Findings

Here, in the end, we shall put together some of the important points emerging from the analysis undertaken in the preceding chapters. Although the findings are based on the data collected from the sample units located in Haryana, these are quite general in their applications not only for the sample size being sufficiently large, but also because it is highly representative of the small-scale units as a whole. For locational and other considerations pointed at the beginning, Haryana is in fact the most ideally suited state for a study of this kind.

It has been observed that sole proprietorship is the most dominant form of ownership/organization in the small-scale sector irrespective of the unit size. It is much more prevalent in the case of units comprising the tiny sector, which we have so far referred to as the small size-group. Partnership form of organization is also quite popular, but more so in the case of medium size units. The joint-stock companies, though quite small in number, are typical of units which are relatively larger in size. Whereas partnership is the most accepted form of organization in chemicals and textiles, sole proprietorship occurs more frequently in the other product-groups.

Majority of the units belonging to all the three size-groups are young (six to ten years) in age. In general a positive relationship is discernible between the age of the firms and their asset size. The engineering group, on the other hand, consists of a large proportion of units which are older (more than 10 years in age) as compared to those producing other products. The chemical and textile units can be said to be 'infant' because most of them are below six years in age.

Further, the joint-stock companies and sole proprietorship firms enjoy a relatively better position in terms of the availability of larger amount of spare funds for marketing activities. Those run on partnership basis, however, appear to be suffering from a disadvantageous position in this regard. Product-wise, the chemical and engineering units have an edge over those comprising the other product-groups.

On an average, each unit offers employment to 18 persons. The capital invested per person indicates that the tiny units offer a relatively greater employment potential than that offered by firms of medium and large size. Among the various product-groups, textile units generate much more employment than others.

The size-wise analysis offers ample evidence to show that large firms prefer to specialize in the production of a limited number of product lines. Again, it is the large firms which produce lesser number of product items than the small ones. The average number of product lines per unit (width of the product-mix) is the highest in metals and the lowest in food-wood. On the other hand, the average number of items per line per unit (depth of the product mix) is maximum in food-wood and minimum in textiles. The relativity between gross profit rate and depth of the product mix in various product-groups is indicative of a positive relationship between the two, and shows that it is the latter which appears to determine the former. The fact that the gross profit rate tends to decline with the increase in the asset-size of the firms, is quite significant. While it is consistent with the depth of the product mix determining the gross profit rate, it also negates the common thinking that smaller units are less profitable than the large ones.

It has been further observed that the majority of the small-scale units do not undertake any activity aimed at product development. The healthy trend, however, is that the proportion of such units declines with the increase in asset size of the firms. Among those engaged in product development, modifying competitors' product and developing own samples are the two most popular product development activities in all the three size-groups. Technical advice is obtained by a very limited number of units of small and medium size, whereas it is quite common in the case of those with large size. Market surveys are rarely conducted for their results to be used as the basis of product development, whatever be the size of the unit. The product-wise analysis reveals a similar position as to the relative use of various product development activities. Developing own samples and modifying competitors' product continue to be the two most popular product development activities in all the product-groups.

Insofar as product bearing ISI mark is a measure of product quality, it seems that maintenance of product quality does not appear to be a matter of much concern, particularly for the smaller (small and medium) units. This is borne out by the fact that the non-users of any quality mark in their case far exceeds the users of ISI mark. The larger units are, however, relatively better off in this regard. Since the use of own quality mark does not serve as a substitute for ISI mark in terms of the users' perceptions of quality, the much wider use of own quality mark as compared to that of the ISI mark does not change the position for the better. However, the consciousness for product quality does seem to have grown with the increase in the asset-size of the firms. This is evident from the fact that the increase in firms' asset-size is associated with an increase in the use of ISI mark on the one hand, and a decline in the non-users of any quality mark on the other hand. The overall outcome remaining the same, marketing of product items without any quality mark is a peculiar feature of the textile units. On the contrary, most of the units manufacturing chemicals sell their products under their 'own quality mark'. Engineering units have achieved an edge over others in the use of ISI mark.

It is revealing that branding is not a popular marketing activity in the small-scale sector. This is particularly true of the tiny sector where the brand non-users are in a larger proportion. The size-wise analysis, however, provides evidence to show that the use of branding gains popularity with the increase in the size of units. The advantages of using family brand have outweighed those of using individual brand so that the former is used more frequently than the latter in all the three size-groups. Branding being the most popular in chemicals, in each of the remaining product-groups firms using family branding outnumber those using individual branding. For obvious reasons, the use of registered brands is more popular than that of unregistered brands in all the size-groups. However, unregistered brands have much wider use in textiles and registered brands in metals.

Inspite of the fact that packaging performs multifarious role in selling, a majority of the units in the small sector, irrespective of the size, does not consider packaging as an important marketing activity. However, since the proportion of units making use of packaging has substantially increased with the increase in the size of units, the use of packaging and the asset-size of the firms are positively related. In other words, it means that packaging does not serve as an important element of the marketing strategy in the case of smaller units. But the larger units do recognize it as an important marketing variable. In terms of product-groups, packaging is most popular in chemicals and least in metals, which is very much in keeping with the broad nature of the products produced in these two product-groups. Since a large number of the chemical units are of medium size, average packaging expenses are obviously the highest there and the lowest in the case of smaller units.

Convenience in handling has been rated as the most important objective of packaging, regardless of the size of the firms. The objectives of product protection and sales by description follow in a descending order of importance, which holds good in the case of units belonging to all the three size-groups. As a means of attracting customers (i.e., product promotion) packaging is treated as the least important. The larger units, of course, do make use of packaging as a means of promotion but only to a limited extent. A similar position obtains from the analysis according to various product-groups. Convenience in handling is the most important objective, followed by product protection, and sales by description. Packaging is aimed at attracting customers by only a few firms producing chemical, engineering, and food-wood products, and by none of the firms manufacturing textile and metal products.

In general, the small industrial units have been found to be facing acute price competition. This is obvious from the fact that 'meeting out competition' continues to be an overriding consideration in price fixation in the case of these units. The tiny units among them fall prey to this problem in much larger number than those of medium and large size. It adds to their misery when these tiny units strive for 'growth in their sales' in the face of keen price competition. The 'target return on sales' as a basis of product pricing tends to become more popular in the case of firms of larger size, since the larger units face relatively less degree of price competition. It is dismal to note that price is never used as a means of 'increasing the market share' by the small-scale units irrespective of their size.

The relative importance of different pricing objectives has not been found materially different among the various product-groups. 'Meeting out competition' remains the most important pricing objective in all the product-groups, except in the case of textiles and metals. 'Target return on sales' is most popular in textiles and 'sales growth' in metals. Conversely, 'sales growth' is least used in textiles and 'target return on sales' in metals.

Among the various factors influencing price-setting, cost of production has emerged as the most important factor, particularly for the tiny units. Competitors' prices have come to be rated as the second most important factor in the case of units of all the three sizes. Consumers' paying capacity has been found to be almost irrelevant to price-setting regardless of size characteristic. Product demand is considered to be of greater relevance in price-setting by the smaller firms and market conditions by the larger firms. It is significant that the relevance of product cost and product demand to price-setting tends to decrease with the increase in the asset size of the firms. The product-wise position is essentially the same with cost of production and competitors' prices being the two most important factors influencing price-setting in all the product-groups. As before, the consumers' paying capacity does not matter in price-setting in any product-group.

As regards the choice between single price policy and multiple price policy, a majority of the units in the three size groups prefers to follow single price policy. The tendency to follow single price policy gets stronger with the increase in asset size of the firms. The outcome of product-wise analysis is not different as single price policy is relatively more popular in all the product-groups, except in engineering.

A large majority of the tiny units as also those of the larger size has adopted prices at par with those of their major competitors. A more significant observation is that the trend of charging prices above the competitive prices tends to become stronger with the increase in the asset size of the firms. This means that large size enables a firm to decide the prices of its product items more independently of the competitive prices, offering it monopolistic advantage in price fixation. The policy of charging competitive prices is most prevalent in each product-group as well. As compared to other product-groups, the chemical units seem to be enjoying a better position in charging monopolistic prices as also those below the competitive prices.

Most of the firms, irrespective of their size, alter their product prices as a result of the price changes effected by their competitors. This is in line with the most prevalent policy of charging prices at par with those of their competitors. Variations in the 'overall trend in market prices' are also almost as greatly responsible for modification in product prices as competitors' prices. The decision to introduce new product(s) in the market, proposal of selling in the new market area(s), and attempts to boost sales are relatively more important in bringing about price changes in the case of units of larger size than those of medium and small size. Product-wise analysis offers almost a similar picture. As is the position according to size, the prices charged by the competitors and the changes in the overall trend in market prices are the two most important factors forcing a firm to change its product price(s) in all the product-groups. Though much less significant as compared to other factors in all the product-groups, selling in the new market area(s) has been a more relevant consideration in modifying product prices for many of the chemical manufacturing units than others.

Regarding various types of discounts offered by the manufacturers with such objectives as increasing sales, speedy realization of trade debts, etc., cash and quantity discounts are the most popular size-wise as well as product-wise. Seasonal discounts are more commonly used in the case of tiny units and those belonging to metals and food-wood firms. Special discounts are offered by a limited number of medium size units and those belonging to metals and food-wood.

Among the three components (advertising, sales promotion, and personal selling) of promotional-mix, advertising has been the most popular and sales promotion the least used, means of promoting sales in the case of tiny units. Sales promotion gets more popular than advertising in the medium and large units. In other words, it means that advertising loses importance in favour of sales promotion in the case of units of larger size. Another noticeable point is that the use of each of the three elements of promotion strategy increases with the increase in the size of units. The relativity among the three size-groups in this regard further shows that the gain in importance of sales promotion is more at the cost of personal selling than advertising. Except for textiles, advertising continues to be the most popular tool of promotion in all the product-groups as well, its use being the highest in chemicals and engineering. Personal selling, on the other hand, is least popular in the case of all product-groupings with its use frequency being the highest in chemicals and lowest in food-wood.

The analysis in terms of the total expenses incurred on each element of promotion policy reveals that on the whole personal selling accounts for the highest proportion of total promotional expenses and sales promotion takes away only a meagre part of the promotional budget. Units of large size offer a different picture insofar as they spend the largest share of their promotional budget on advertising and the lowest on sales promotion. The earlier conclusion that advertising and sales promotion tend to gain importance at the cost of personal selling is reinforced by the fact that its relative share in the promotional budget experiences a decline with the increase in the asset size of the firms. It is indeed discouraging to note that on an average each firm of even large size incurs only a very small fraction (0.93%) of their sales on promotion, the lowest being 0.64% in the medium size units.

Except for engineering and food-wood products, personal selling accounts for the highest proportion of promotional expenses and sales promotion the lowest in the remaining product groups. In relation to total sales, promotional expenses per unit are the highest (1.78%) in chemicals and the lowest (0.13%) in food-wood. Interestingly, the relative share of advertising is the highest in engineering and that of sales promotion in food-wood. A more significant outcome is that promotional expenses explain variations in sales to the extent of 9 percent. Yet correlation coefficient reveals that there is a significant association between promotional effort and sales revenue.

As regards the choice among the three commonly used methods of deciding advertising budget, the smaller units have greater preference for the 'affordable' method. The 'competitive parity' method is most popular in the medium-size units and the 'percentage of sales' method in the large units. The use frequency of the *competitive parity* method is the lowest in the case of large units where *affordable method* is not at all used which is due largely to lack of sales planning. The *percentage of sales* method, on the other hand, is least used in the small and medium size-groups. Among the various product-groups, the affordable method has the highest use in engineering and the lowest in chemicals. Whereas chemical units enjoy the distinction of making the maximum use of percentage of sales method, the competitive parity method is most preferred by the units manufacturing textiles and metals.

Advertising is undertaken mainly with a view to creating brand awareness and achieving higher sales/profit. While the large units make use of advertising primarily to build up, the tiny units strive more for higher sales. The two objectives, namely, neutralizing competitors advertising and introducing new item(s) in the market receive more attention from the units of large size than those of smaller and medium size. Increasing sales/profit and creating brand awareness continue to be the most popular advertising objectives in all the product-groups as well, especially in chemicals and engineering. Incidentally, it is in the case of chemical and engineering units that neutralizing competitors' advertising and selling in the new market area(s) are also relatively more popular than elsewhere. Advertising as a means of introducing new item(s) in the market is the least important objective in all the units irrespective of what product they produce.

The overall media use pattern is the same in all the units irrespective of their size. The distinctive feature is that the newspapers and magazines are the two most commonly used media. Barring a few units manufacturing chemicals, radio and television have not so far been accepted as a means to promote sales. Except for wall-writings and posters, the dependence on out-door hoardings and direct mail (including letter-writing and directories/cinema slides) has risen significantly with the increase in the size of firms. The media-mix varies significantly with the type of product produced and marketed by a firm particularly in respect of the use of newspapers and magazines. In addition to having attained maximum popularity in all the product-groups, these two media have the highest use frequency in engineering and the lowest in food-wood. Other media are much less important, and the variations in their usage among the various product-groups are much less pronounced than those in the case of newspapers and magazines.

Whereas the effectiveness of advertising largely depends on how best the advertising message is developed, it is disappointing to note that an overwhelming number of units belonging to each size-group and product-group prepare their advertising messages without making any reference to specialized agencies/professionals. But keeping in view the importance of their role in producing more appealing and effective advertising message, the larger units are making a greater use of the services provided by these specialized agencies. Nature of the product produced does not change the overall picture in this regard. However, the use of specialized agencies is much more popular in the chemical and engineering units than those producing other products. It has been observed that advertising coverage in the case of majority of the units is aimed at reaching the local market only. Advertising directed to gain access to international market is undertaken by a very small number of units at the overall level. The proportion of such units is the highest in the case of large units. Whereas local market is typically the target of advertising for the tiny units, the focus of advertising in the case of large units is on tapping the national market. A more visible point of difference is the increasing national and international coverage and the declining local and regional coverage, as the asset-size of the firms tends to increase.

Product-wise analysis shows that advertising at the national level is most widely used in chemicals and engineering. While advertising aimed at regional coverage is least popular with the engineering firms, advertising for tapping local demand is most popular in metals and food-wood. Understandably, there is no international coverage of advertising in chemicals, food-wood, and metals.

Inspite of the important role which personal selling can play in the generation of sales, salesmen are employed by a very limited number of firms of all the three sizes. The redeeming feature, however, is the increasing recourse to utilizing the services of salesmen as the firms grow in their asset-size. The proportion of firms using personal selling in their promotional mix is much lower than of those not using it, in all the product-groups except chemicals. As regards the various functions which sales force is expected to perform, it is significant to note that firms of all sizes make use of the services of sales force primarily with a view to seeking sales orders and collecting payments. Utilizing salesmen for gathering marketing information comes next in order of importance. Product-wise also the order of importance of the various objectives remains the same as in the case of size-wise analysis.

Sales promotion (selling activities of non-recurring nature) is considered to be a more popular means of promotion in the case of firms of medium and large size. Majority of the units in all the three size-groups resort to distribution of free gifts/samples. Other sales promotion activities such as participation in trade fairs, cooperative advertising, and special discounts are being used by a very limited number of firms, irrespective of their size. Sales promotion activities are, however, most popular in chemicals and least so in metals, whereas free gifts/samples are allowed by almost all the textile units.

Channel decisions are the most crucial in the area of distribution. It is significant that as many as 40 per cent of the units at the overall level are not using any well-defined distribution channel. Among the channel users, the zero-level channel is the most popular in all the size-groups. This means that as the circumstances are such or otherwise, product distribution in the small sector is dominated by direct selling. A relatively greater use of both zero-level and one-level channel by the larger units indicates that these units have an in-built preference for shorter channels. Engineering units make the most use of zero-level channel, apparently due to considerations of the technical nature of the products, reliability, and users' specifications. Compared with other product-groups, there is a relatively greater use of longer channels in the textile units which appears to be due to the product items being 'shopping item' of mass consumption.

Size-wise analysis of distribution intensity reveals that the increase in the size of the firms is associated with an increase in the use of exclusive distribution and a decline in mass distribution. Barring engineering units, mass distribution system has been found to be most popular in all the product-groups, especially textiles. The selective distribution is used by a relatively greater number of textile and chemical units as compared to those manufacturing other products.

The selection of middlemen who assist in the flow of product(s) from the producers to the ultimate consumers/users, is affected by a number of factors. Among these factors, the goodwill of the middlemen is considered to be the most important one. Whereas the consideration of sound financial position of the middlemen occupies the second place in order of importance, availability of warehousing facility with the middlemen is rated to be least relevant. The size-wise analysis further reveals that the consideration of offer of promotional support has an edge over that of sound financial position of the middlemen in the case of larger units. The various factors affecting the choice of middlemen follow the same order of importance in all the product-groups as well. However, the consideration of offer of promotional support having an edge over sound financial position holds goods only in the case of food-wood products.

Since market performance of a product is determined to a large extent by the interest and involvement of the middlemen in pushing through the product, it is necessary that the middlemen engaged in the distribution are the motivated people. Among the various types of facilities and incentives which are extended by the manufacturers to attract the right type of middlemen into the job, easy credit terms is the most popular incentive in the case of units of all the three sizes. It is, followed, in a descending order, by the incentive of replacement of defective items, cooperative advertising, free gifts, and special discounts. The incentives of cooperative advertising and replacement of defective items tend to become less important with the increase in the asset size of the firms. The benefit of easy credit term is the most widely used incentive in all the product-groups. The incentive of replacement of defective items is at the second place everywhere, except chemicals. Offer of easy credit is most popular in textiles, facility to replace the defective items in metals, and cooperative advertising in chemicals.

The importance of sales forecasting for any business organization, whether small or large, cannot be underestimated. It provides the essential basis for planning and implementation of suitable marketing policies and programmes in all the areas, be it product, pricing, promotion, or distribution. It is in keeping with the importance of forecasting that a large majority of units in all the three size-groups have been found to be undertaking sales forecasting. Past behaviour of sales is the most widely used basis of making sales forecast in each size-group. Only occassionally are the sales force estimates used for future projections of sales. Past behaviour of sales is the most preferred basis of forecasting in the case of tiny units, which loses its significance substantially with the increase in the size of the units. Forecasting based on overall market trend has gained prominence in the case of large units. Product-wise position is essentially the same. Past behaviour of sales is most widely used in all the product-groups, particularly in metals. Sales force estimates are the least used everywhere, particularly in textiles and food-wood.

Market segmentation is an important marketing tool insofar as it helps the management to tailor its marketing programmes to suit the needs of buyers. Almost totally unaware of market segmentation, all firms have revealed the geographic coverage of their market only in terms of District, State, Country as a whole, or foreign countries. Although this kind of geographic coverage is different from geographic segmentation, the analysis even on these lines throws up some interesting results. For example, the proportion of units having national coverage is the lowest. The tiny units have the highest local coverage, whereas medium and large units receive the highest position in national coverage. It is also quite significant that the local coverage declines and international coverage increases with the increase in the asset size of the firms. Among the various product-groups, local and state coverage both are the highest in food-wood, national coverage in chemicals, and international coverage in textiles. Chemicals, textiles, and metals are the three product-groups which have maximum national coverage.

The facility of credit sales is treated as a convenient means of increasing sales in the small-scale sector. It is an interesting phenomenon that extending the facility of credit sales is almost a sort of compulsion for most of them. The reason being that anyone who denies this facility faces the problem of reduction in sales due to severe competition. As compared to the smaller units, the proportion of credit sales is much heavier in the case of large units. Except for food-wood, the proportion of units allowing substantial credit sales is the highest in all the product-groups. In the case of food-wood, on the other hand, a substantial number of firms do not permit credit sales.

The decisions affecting the planning of marketing mix relate either to product, price, promotion, distribution, or any combination of them. Interestingly, product decisions have been rated as the most important irrespective of the asset size of the firms. Pricing decisions which occupy the second position, are followed by distribution decisions in the case of small as well as medium units, but these are least important for the large units. Although least important for the small and medium units, the promotional decisions are as important as the pricing decisions for the large units. Product decisions have been rated as the most important by majority of the units belonging to all the product-groups. Pricing decisions come next in the case of metals and food-wood, and distribution decisions in the case of chemicals and textiles. Promotional decisions are considered most important only by a few firms in all the product-groups.

8.1 IMPLICATIONS

The crux of the entire discussion is that the small-scale industries in Haryana are very backward in developing a suitable marketing culture for themselves. This is particularly true of those marketing activities which directly affect the saleability and the overall market demand for their products. Their ability to grow into more viable concerns is greatly circumscribed by the limited *demand cake* for which many of them compete rather closely to have a better part of it. Neither individually nor collectively they are in a position to finance on a continuous basis the magnitude of marketing effort needed for enlarging the size of the cake. The result is that the endeavours of these units to grow in size and scale become the first victim of the operation of a kind of vicious circle emanating from the limited size of the demand cake. It so operates that the smaller the cake, the smaller the sales — the smaller the sales, the limited the financial resources to spare for the marketing activities necessary to increase the size of the cake.

While the small-scale sector as a whole is in the grip of this vicious circle, the grip tends to become tighter in its effects in the case of the smaller of the small units. Given the circumstances and the overall environment in which they operate, to think of panacea is indeed too much. However, a few suggestions crop up which may be helpful in improving their marketing culture and thus breaking this vicious circle. These are of general nature applicable to all units irrespective of their size and the nature of product produced.

Product as a larger package of the core product combined with quality, branding, and packaging offers much scope for improvement. Apart from the need to popularize and strengthen the overall product development activity, it will be highly useful that the small-scale units assign greater importance to the role of technical advice and market surveys in developing new products as well as modifying the existing ones. Knowing through market surveys what the market can accept and then having the demand characteristics translated into the product will enable them to achieve the much needed matching of products with markets and enhancing the saleability of their products.

Product quality has not been a matter of serious concern for the small units. Since product quality is the most essential ingredient which commands customers' faith in the product, it is imperative that these units standardize their products in keeping with the users' needs and make efforts to qualify for the use of ISI mark. Those engaged in the manufacturing of textiles, metals and engineering goods ought to fulfil this requirement more earnestly than others.

Even if a product makes an excellent match with market requirements, still it hasn't quite a reliable existence unless it is given a brand name. Since branding has not been very popular particularly with the smaller units, any marketing action plan will be more effective in achieving greater market penetration if branding is accepted as an essential marketing activity.

The role of packaging has also not been adequately recognized as a necessary tool for promotion and product differentiation. The state of art of packaging will help in improving physical distribution and in crossing the barriers on the sale of products. Moreover, packaging has to be accepted as a necessary ingredient of the promotion strategy, more as a means of communicating with the customers rather than treating it as an evil involving expense.

Among the three elements of promotion mix, in general there is a definite case for a relatively greater emphasis on advertising than personal selling. Advertising copy and the message intended to be conveyed to the prospectives should be got designed and prepared from professional agencies and directed to neutralizing competition and increasing sales. The selection of media vehicle (even among various newspapers and magazines) should be guided by the consideration of creating and enlarging demand. To accomplish all this bare minimum, the small-scale industries will have to raise their promotion budget, which, in terms of percentage to sales, is now at the rock bottom. The various sales promotion activities also call for much greater emphasis than what it has been so far. If accorded due place in the promotion mix, these can serve as effective means of increasing sales especially in the case of the tiny units.

These industries will do well in evolving a suitable marketing culture if they take steps to streamline the distribution path for their products. This will facilitate identification of the right type of middlemen to be involved in the process of distribution. The selection of middlemen is a crucial decision because of the powerful influence which they exert in determining the relative importance to be given to other elements of the marketing mix. In view of the limited financial resources of these industries, the selection of middlemen should be made keeping in view the financial support which they can extend and their willingness in pushing through the product(s).

The widely prevailing practice of charging competitive prices does not leave enough room for using pricing as a means of increasing the market share or the size of the demand cake. The price changes as and when effected are necessitated more by the changes in competitive prices than by decisions of selling in the new market area(s) or of boosting sales. In these circumstances there is hardly any freedom left for manipulating prices in working out an appropriate sales/marketing strategy. The same is also true of channel decisions. The market coverage being largely local or regional, the distribution channel has necessarily to be the shortest. Given these two constraints, product and promotion are the only two operative elements which can be used with some freedom in designing a marketing mix appropriate to the needs and circumstances of each size-group and product-group. However, the success of a marketing strategy based largely on these two elements requires the much needed segmentation of the market. Since this has been practically non-existent till now, it is highly desirable that the small-scale units continuously engage themselves in the process of market segmentation on appropriate lines and incorporate a thrust in their promotion mix accordingly.

Annexure

Questionnaire

---

1. GENERAL INFORMATION

1.1 a) Name and qualifications of the respondent ________________
____

b) Name and address of the firm
____
____
____
____

1.2 Year of establishment

1.3 Form of organization

a) Sole proprietorship ( )
b) Partnership ( )
c) Public or private company ( )
d) Any other (specify) ( )

1.4 Give the following information regarding the number of persons working in your concern.

a) Manager/supervisors (including the owner) ( )
b) Non-managerial staff (office clerks, salesmen, etc.) ( )
c) Others (workers, sweepers,

gate-keepers, etc.) ( )
Total ( )

1.5 State the number of persons in your sales department and their monthly total salary.

	Total number	*Total salary*
a) Salesmen	( )	( )
b) Sales manager(s)	( )	( )

1.6 State the value (Rs.) of gross capital employed.

a) Land and buildings ( )
b) Plant and machinery ( )
c) Stock, cash, B/R, debtors, etc. ( )

1.7 State the major product items that are being manufactured by your firm.

a) ( ) b) ( )
c) ( ) d) ( )

1.8 How do you rank the following decisions in order of importance?
(assign rank order by writing 1,2,3,. . . . .)

a) Product decisions ( )
b) Advertising decisions ( )
c) Pricing decisions ( )
d) Distribution/channel decisions ( )

1.9 State the volume of your sales during the last two years.

(Rs. in lac)

	1986–87	*1985–86*
a) In domestic market	( )	( )
b) In foreign market	( )	( )

1.10 i) Do you make an estimate of future sales?

YES/NO

ii) If yes, which of the following basis do you use?

a) Discussion with buyers ( )

b) Sales force estimates ( )

c) Overall market trend ( )

d) Past sales behaviour ( )

e) Government policies ( )

1.11 What is your target market (area–wise)?
Local/State/Regional/National/International

2. PRODUCT

2.1 While developing new items or modifying the existing ones, which of the following methods do you use?

a) Develop own samples/models ( )

b) Modify competitor's product ( )

c) Consult technical experts ( )

d) Conduct market survey(s) ( )

2.2 Which of the following mark do you use?

a) ISI mark ( )

b) Own mark ( )

c) No mark is used ( )

2.3 i) Do you sell your products under any specific brand name?

YES/NO

ii) If yes, state the brand name for each product item.

	Product item	Brand Name
a)	__________	__________
b)	__________	__________
c)	__________	__________

d) ______ ______

2.4 Do you have any registered trade mark?

YES/NO

2.5 i) Is packaging an important marketing activity in your case?

YES/NO

ii) If yes, which of the following objectives do you intend to achieve through packaging?

a) Convenience in handling ( )
b) Product protection ( )
c) Sales by description ( )
d) Attracting customers ( )

2.6 How much, on an average, are your annual expenses on packaging?

Rs.______

3. PRICING

3.1 How do you rank the following pricing objectives? (assign rank order by writing 1,2,3, ...)

a) Target return on sales ( )
b) Meeting competition ( )
c) Sales growth ( )
d) Increasing market share ( )

3.2 Which of the following factors do you consider important in deciding the selling price of your product items?

a) Cost of production ( )
b) Product demand ( )
c) Competitors' prices ( )
d) Market conditions ( )
e) Consumer paying capacity ( )

3.3 Which of the following alternative pricing policies do you generally use?

a) Single price policy ( )

b) Multiple price policy ( )

3.4 How do you fix the prices of your products as compared to those of your major competitors?

Below ( )

Above ( )

At par ( )

3.5 How frequently have the following factors led to refixation of the prices of your product(s)?

	Generally	*Occasionally*	*Never*
a) Change in major competitor's prices	( )	( )	( )
b) Change in the overall trend in market prices	( )	( )	( )
c) Decisions to introduce new items	( )	( )	( )
d) Selling in the new market	( )	( )	( )
e) Boosting sales	( )	( )	( )

3.6 What is the average gross margin charged by you?

____

3.7 How much of the following discounts do you offer?

	%age to sale price
a) Quantity discounts	( )
b) Cash discounts	( )
c) Seasonal discounts	( )
d) Trade discount	( )
e) Special discounts	( )

4. PROMOTION

4.1 i) Are you engaged in advertising?

YES/NO

ii) If yes, on which of the following basis do you generally decide your advertising budget?

	Generally	*Occasionally*	*Never*
a) Capacity to afford	( )	( )	( )
b) Percentage of sales	( )	( )	( )
c) Promotional expenses by competitors	( )	( )	( )

4.2 Which of the following are your advertising objectives?

	Always	*Sometimes*	*Never*
a) Increasing sales/profit	( )	( )	( )
b) Creating brand awareness	( )	( )	( )
c) Neutralizing competitors' advertising	( )	( )	( )
d) Introducing new item(s) in the market	( )	( )	( )
e) Selling in new market area(s)	( )	( )	( )

4.3 How much, on an average, do you spend on the following advertising media per annum?

	(Rs.)
a) Radio/TV	( )
b) Newspapers/magazines	( )
c) Wall-writing/posters/handbills	( )
d) Outdoor hoardings or bill boarder	( )
e) Direct mail/letter writing	( )
f) Directories, cinema slides, etc.	( )
g) Any other	( )
Total	( )

4.4 Who prepares advertising message for you?
- a) Self/own staff ( )
- b) Advertising agency/professional artists ( )

4.5 State your advertising coverage.
- a) Local ( )
- b) Regional ( )
- c) National ( )
- d) International ( )

4.6 Which of the following functions the salesmen are required to perform?
- a) Seeking orders ( )
- b) Providing delivery ( )
- c) Collecting payments ( )
- d) Introducing new items to dealers/customers ( )
- e) Gathering market information ( )

4.7 How much, on an average, do you spend on the following sales promotion activities?

(Rs.)

- a) Free gifts/samples ( )
- b) Participation in trade fairs/ exhibitions ( )
- c) Cooperative advertising ( )
- d) Special discounts ( )

4.8 What percentage of total sales do you attribute to credit sales?
- a) Below 25% ( )
- b) 25% to 50% ( )
- c) Above 50% ( )

5. DISTRIBUTION

5.1 To which of the following (distribution) channel members do you generally sell?

a) Final consumers ( )

b) Agents ( )

c) Wholesalers ( )

d) Retailers ( )

5.2 Which distribution system do you follow?

a) Selling through every possible outlet/channel ( )

b) Selling through selected dealers ( )

c) Selling through one dealer in one city/area ( )

5.3 Which of the following factors do you consider important while selecting middlemen/agents?

a) Goodwill ( )

b) Financial position ( )

c) Promotional support to the product ( )

d) Cost of using middleman ( )

e) Warehousing facilities ( )

5.4 To what extent the following activities are undertaken in order to win dealers' support?

	Generally	*Occasionally*	*Never*
a) Free gifts	( )	( )	( )
b) Cooperative advertising	( )	( )	( )
c) Special discounts	( )	( )	( )
d) Easy credit terms	( )	( )	( )
e) Replacement of defective items	( )	( )	( )

5.5 Give the following information in respect of inventories:

Inventory	*Value (Rs.)*
a) Average	( )
b) Minimum stock	( )
c) Maximum stock	( )

Bibliography

1. Ahmad, Nisar, Problems and Management of Small Scale and Cottage Industry, Deep and Deep Publications, Delhi, 1987.
2. Bal Krishan, G., Financing of Small Scale Industries in India, Gokhale Institute of Politics and Economics, Poona, 1962.
3. Basu, S.K., Place and Problems of Small Scale Industries, A. Mukherjee & Co, Calcutta, 1957.
4. Battacharya, H., Entrepreneur Banker and Small Scale Industry, Deep & Deep Publications, New Delhi
5. Bhandari, P. M., A Handbook of Small Scale Industries, The Peerlen publishers, Calcutta, 1975.
6. Chatterjee, A. K., Small Scale industries and Public Sector in India , Role of State Sector in Developing Countries (Ed), People's Publishing House, Delhi.
7. Desai, Vasant, Small Scale Industries – Problems and Prospects: Karnataka Chamber of Commerce.
8. __, Organization and Management of Small Scale Industries, Himalaya Publishing House, New Delhi, 1979.
9. Deshpande, M. U., Entrepreneurship of Small Scale Industries—Concept, Growth, Management, Deep and Deep Publications, New Delhi.
10. Dhar, P. N., Some Aspects of Technical Progress in Small Scale Industries, *Indian Economic Review*, Vol 3, No.1, Feb. 1956.
11. Dhar, P. N. and Lydal, H.F., The Role of Small Enterprise in Indian Economic Development, Asia Publishing House, 1971.

12. Dua, D. R., Small Industries and Handicrafts, Delhi, Survodya Publications, 1967.
13. Fajardo, H. R., Management Problems in Small Scale Industries, *Small Industry Journal*, Vol 5, No. 4, April – May – June 1973.
14. Farooquee, Q. H., Small Scale and Cottage Industries as a Means of Providing Better Opportunities for Labour in India, A. M. U., Aligarh, 1958.
15. Ford Foundation, Development of Small Scale Industries in India—Prospects, Problems and Policies, Ford Foundation, New Delhi.
16. Goyal S.K. et.al., Studies in National Development, Small Scale Sector and Big Business, Corporate Studies Group, IIPA, New Delhi, 1984.
17. Gupta, K., Small Scale Industries, Dehati Pustak Bhandar, Delhi, 1962.
18. Hoselitz, B. F. (Ed.), The Role of Small Industry in the Process of Economic Growth, Mouton, the Hague and Paris, 1968.
19. Jain, O. P., Small Industry Exports, S. Chand & Co, Delhi, 1971.
20. Lakshman, T. K., Problems and Prospects of Ancilliary Industries in a Growing Economy, Rekha, Bangalore, 1970.
21. Mahendra, K. L., Small Scale Industries and the Public Sector–Role of State Sector in Developing Countries (Ed.), Peoples Publishing House, Delhi,1977.
22. Malhotra, D. K., Role of Small Industries in National Development, *Yojana*, Vol.6, No. 15, Aug 1962.
23. Merani, S. T., Reflections on Development of Small Scale Industries, *Productivity*, Vol. 6, No 1, Spring, 1965.
24. Mohan, K. K., Small Industry Enterprise Handbook, Productivity Service International, Bombay, 1971.
25. Mitra, L. K., Employment and Output in Small Enterprises, Asia, 1961.
26. Nanjundappa, D. M., Planning for Small Industries: Some Suggestions, *The Economic Times*, Vol.6, Oct.10,1966.
27. Narula. B. S., Development of Small Industries: Some Suggestions, *The Economic Times*, Vol. 6, Oct. 10, 1966.
28. Oliver, Rober W., The Role of Small Scale Manufacturing in Economic Development, Washington DC,1966.

29. Philip, A. M., Small Enterprise Development, Policies and Programmes, Management Development Services, No. 14, ILO, Geneva, 1977.

30. Rao, M. V., Problems of Development of Small Scale Enterprises as Ancilliary to Large Concerns, 1962.

31. Rao, R. V., Cottage and Small Scale Industries and Planned Economy, Sterling Publishers Pvt. Ltd., New Delhi, 1967.

32. ___, Small Industries and Development Economy in India, Concept Publishing Company, New Delhi, 1978.

33. Report of Administrative Reforms Commission, Report on Small Scale Sector (Mimeographed), New Delhi, 1969.

34. Report – Govt. of India., Small Scale Industries in Perspective, Development Commissioner, New Delhi, 1968.

35. ___, Report of Steering Committee for Export promotion in Small Scale Sector, New Delhi, 1981.

36. ___, Working Groups on Five Year Plan for Small Scale Industries, Development Commissioner, Small Scale Industries, Mimeographed, New Delhi.

37. ___, Sources of Marketing Assistance to Small Scale Industries, Internal Marketing, Royal Printing Works, New Delhi, 1977.

38. ___, Facilities for Development of Small Scale Industries, Royal Printing Press, New Delhi, 1977.

39. Report of Ministry of Industrial Development, Report of the Committee for Drafting Legislation for Small Scale Industries (Mimeographed), New Delhi, 1972.

40. Report of Ministry of Industrial Development, Development Commissioner (SSI), Small Scale Industries: Twenty Five Years of Progress, New Delhi, 1973.

41. Sapru, K. N., Marketing Problems of Small Industries in Marketing in India– Cases and Readings by S. Neelamegham (Ed.), Vikas, New Delhi, 1988

42. Sharma, A. P., Marketing Problems of Small Scale Industries in Marketing in India–Cases and Readings by S. Neelamegham (Ed.),Vikas, New Delhi, 1988.

43. Sharma, G. D., How to Start Your Own Small Scale Industry, Vision Books, New Delhi, 1984.

44. Shashi Bala, Management of Small Scale Industries, Deep and Deep Publications, Delhi, 1984.

45. Singh, Baljit, The Economics of Small Scale Industries: A Case Study of Small Scale Establishments of Moradabad,

Asia, Bombay 1961.

46. Singh, Charan, India's Economic Policy: The Gandhian Blueprint, Vikas, New Delhi, 1978.
47. Singh, N. N., Scientific Management of Small Scale Industries, Lalvani Publishing House, New Delhi.
48. Singh R. and Agnihotri, A. K., Marketing of Machine Tools in Small Sector, Small Enterprises Development, *Management and Extension Journal,* Vol 16, No. 4, Dec. 1989.
49. Stepanek. J. E., Managers for Small Industry, Asia, Bombay, 1962.
50. Tambi, J. M. L., Marketing Strategy for Small Scale Industries in Marketing in India—Cases and Readings by S. Neelamegham (Ed.), Vikas, New Delhi, 1988.
51. ___, Strategy for Development of Backward Area, *Financial Express,* Aug 23, 1974.
52. Thapar, S. D., Small Industries in India, Osaka.
53. Tulsi, S. K., Incentives for Small Scale Industries—An Evaluation, Economic and Scientific Research Foundation, Delhi (Mimeographed).
54. Tyabji, Nasir, The Small Industries Policy in India, Oxford University Press, New Delhi, 1989.
55. UNESCO Research Centre on Social and Economic Development in Southern Asia, Social Aspects of Small Industries in India, United India Press, New Delhi, 1962.
56. ___, Small Industries and Social Change, United India Press, New Delhi, 1966.
57. Vepa, R. K., Small Industry – The Challenge of the Eighties, Vikas Publishing House Pvt. Ltd., New Delhi.

Index

Ambala, 7, 11
Bhiwani, 11
Faridabad, 11
Gram Udyog Mandal, 14
Gurgoan, 11
Haryana State Small-Scale
  Industries and Export Corporation, 11
Hissar, 11
ISI (Indian Standards Institute)
  mark, 34, 35, 36, 37, 122, 123
Indian Army, 7
Industrial Policy Resolution of 1948, 2
Industrial Policy Resolution of 1956, 3
Industrial Policy Statement of 6 April 1948, 3
Industrial Policy Statement of 1977, 3
Jind, 11
Karnal, 11
Khadi and Village Industries Board, 2
Kurukshetra, 11
Mahendergarh, 11
National Small-Scale Industries Corporation, 2
Panipat, 7
Rohtak, 11
Sirsa, 11
Working Group on Small-Scale Industries, 6
World Bank Report, 1
Yamuna Nagar, 7